UFO Briefing Book

A Guide to
Congressional Oversight
of the UAP Phenomenon

James P. Lough

outskirts
press

Outskirts Press, Inc.
http://www.outskirtspress.com

ISBN: 978-1-9772-4090-3

Outskirts Press and the "OP" logo are trademarks belonging to Outskirts Press, Inc.

PRINTED IN THE UNITED STATES OF AMERICA

TABLE OF CONTENTS

ABOUT THE AUTHOR

JAMES P. LOUGH IS a retired attorney who specialized in government law, including constitutional law, election law and appellate practice. He also taught *"Decision Making in Urban Communities"* at the San Diego State University School of Public Affairs. His interest in UFOs comes from having witnessed several at close range over his lifetime. He resides in Southern California with his wife and mother.

SEPT. 3, 2021

J + M

IF YOU CAN'T SLEEP,

READ THIS

Jim Leugh

ACKNOWLEDGMENTS

THERE ARE MANY WHO contributed valuable input to this book. Some cannot be named due to the subject matter with its historic stigma. It would damage their careers. However, those listed are among many who provided advice and encouragement that have made this work possible.

My editor, George Verongos, provided valuable assistance that helped me transition from writing government reports and legal briefs to writing for publication. Mary Margaret Dyer, Lucinda Morel, David Kelly Johnson, Alfonso Martinez, Mary Martinez, Charylene McCain and Kimberly Trotman gave needed support to this effort and I will be forever grateful.

Donald Schmitt (*Coverup at Roswell* (2017)) provided valuable guidance and encouragement throughout the writing process. Captain (ret.) Robert Salas (*Faded Giant* (2005)) provided input on the implications of UFO intrusions at nuclear weapons facilities. In addition, Robert Hastings (*UFOs and Nukes* (2008)) contributed in many ways during the preparation of this book. These three authors' books are mandatory reading for those who wish to gain insight into the long and complicated history of UFO interactions with our nuclear arsenal.

Retired attorney Terry Lovelace shared many insights as both an author and as a former paramedic in the Air Force. He was treated with contempt after experiencing a close encounter while off duty. His book, *Incident at Devil's Den* (2018), chronicles the improper tactics used by our government to separate and punish UFO witnesses, after his 1975 encounter. Military veteran and History Professor Dr. Bruce Solheim (*Timeless* (2018)) also guided me with his historical and military insights.

Yvonne Smith (*Coronado* (2014)) assisted in research and provided valuable perspective during the book's development. Debra Kauble (*Extraordinary Contact* (2021)) also provided support, being one who has been in the harsh spotlight surrounding this phenomenon. In their books, Yvonne and Debra offer an excellent window into the reality of human interactions with entities who are not of this world.

I

EXECUTIVE SUMMARY

ON JUNE 8, 2020, the Senate Select Intelligence Committee unanimously requested the Director of National Intelligence (DNI) to consult with the Secretary of Defense (SecDef) in order to prepare a report on the activities of the Navy's Unidentified Anomalous Phenomenon Task Force. The UAP Task Force was requested to prepare a unified approach, across the defense and intelligence communities, to respond to unknown phenomenon. This phenomenon was displayed in three declassified videos taken in 2004 and 2015 by Naval flight personnel. The first incident was off the Pacific Coast and involved the Nimitz Carrier Group. The other videos were taken off the Atlantic Coast by elements of the Roosevelt Carrier Group. The videos showed objects which possess flight characteristics that cannot be performed by any known terrestrial aircraft.

This *UFO Briefing Book: A Guide to Congressional Oversight of the UAP Phenomenon* analyzes the specific requests for information to be supplied to the Senate and House Select Intelligence and Armed Services Committees. The request is triggered by the passage of the successor bill to Senate 3905, Intelligence Authorization Act for Fiscal

Year 2021. The language was contained in the committee comments but *not* in the bill's actual text. The main issue is whether these UFO/UAPs[1] present a "threat" to the United States. If the "threat" is real, the report should include recommendations of how Congress should respond. Senate Intel also commends the Office of Naval Intelligence for its efforts to understand the UFO/UAP phenomenon and requests that it establish protocols for other service branches and the intelligence community.

While this briefing book is prepared and supported by many who consider the main source of the UFO/UAP phenomenon to be nonterrestrial, the briefing book's purpose is not to advocate any source of the phenomenon. Its purpose is to give the Armed Services and Select Intelligence Committees information and historical perspective to help Congress assume its proper role of oversight for the activities of the federal government regardless of the source of UFO/UAPs. As the originator of all funding and legal requirements applicable to federal operations, Congress has both the right and the duty to ensure that the government operates efficiently and appropriately.

After this overview, Section II will discuss the basics of the Senate Intel Committee request. In Section III, this book goes into more detail about the eight specific questions that the Senate Intel Committee asked. Most of these questions relate to the concern that these vehicles defy our understanding of the laws of physics and outperform our military assets. If hostile, the objects undermine the defense of the United States. This concern is well-founded but may have unintended consequences in a search for understanding of the phenomenon.

The main concern is whether any terrestrial adversary has achieved a great leap in technology that gives them an undeniable advantage. Since the initial video showing these capabilities was taken in 2004, any terrestrial adversary possessing these vehicles has at least a two-decade technological head start. However, there is no current indication

---

1   For clarity sake, the term UFO that was coined by the Air Force and UAP, which is a recent rebranding of the phenomenon, will be combined (UFO/UAP).

that any country possesses this technology. Our two biggest adversaries, Russia and China, are highly unlikely to have developed the vehicles that caused the 2004 Nimitz Carrier Group incident. Neither had the infrastructure to research and develop the dozens of vehicles seen on radar and visually by trained military personnel over 16 years ago.

China was still emerging from its self-imposed isolation and did not have a research and development capacity to even rival U.S. R & D efforts, let alone make such a massive technological leap. Russia was still emerging from the breakup of the Soviet Union and needed to rely on the United States to help it secure nuclear weapons.

Russia's economy was heavily dependent on hydrocarbon recovery. With the wide swings in the energy market, it would have been difficult for the Russian economy to support the massive research efforts necessary. Absent classified information to the contrary, neither had the infrastructure to develop and deploy dozens of these objects by November 2004.

If Congress is to consider these intrusions to be a terrestrial threat, more information is needed to tie UFO/UAPs to a source. A report to Congress that finds these vehicles are a terrestrial-based threat must include specific evidence tying the vehicles to a specific country. Failure to provide even minimal evidence of a terrestrial source will allow the defense/intelligence communities to continue to hide evidence about the UFO/UAP phenomenon behind compartmentalized, classified programs. All without giving Congress evidence that supports these programs.

Section IV adds some historical context to the UFO/UAP phenomenon including congressional involvement. In many respects, the UFO/UAPs seen by personnel in the Nimitz and Roosevelt Carrier Groups are no different than the "foo fighters" witnessed by World War II pilots. While the military studied the "foo fighter" phenomenon, there are no declassified records of the conclusions reached. Later, in 1947, the United States experienced a "flying saucer wave" but, starting in 1948 there was a decline in sightings until 1952. In

1952, the country had another "wave," including multiple sightings over Washington D.C. In response, the CIA formed the Robertson Panel, composed of military scientists. The panel found that people who witnessed UFO/UAPs were either mistaken, lying, or delusional. They recommended that UFO/UAPs be "debunked" and that groups that studied them should be "watched." After the panel, the Air Force implemented regulations that prevented commercial pilots from talking to the press about UFO/UAP sightings. The Air Force also sent public relations personnel around the country to ridicule people who had sightings. Each of these policies was intended to suppress evidence about the UFO/UAP phenomenon. Much of today's confusion is a result of these efforts.

Against this backdrop, Congress has made few attempts to learn about the phenomenon. The Air Force and CIA, according to declassified records, have taken steps to prevent Congress from taking UFO/UAPs seriously. Except for one short hearing in 1968, no congressional committee has held any open hearings about the issue. Since 1955, when Senator Richard Russell refused to publicly discuss his own sighting in the U.S.S.R., members of Congress have either shied away from the topic or have been rebuffed in their inquiries about it.

Starting in World War II, UFO/UAPs have been seen by military personnel. For the most part, the phenomenon has observed military operations, but has not engaged in any directly aggressive behavior. Observation seems to be the purpose of most of these UFO/UAP-military encounters. However, there has been a significant exception that involves our nuclear weapons. A series of incidents, possibly starting in 1966, have occurred where UFO/UAPs have been seen close to ICBM missile silos. During these incidents, the missile functions were tampered with in a way that shut down entire flights of ICBMs. When defense contractors ran tests on the systems, there was nothing to indicate an internal system fault. There are reports out of post-Soviet Union Russia that similar events occurred at their missile silos.

Except for the tampering with the operating systems, there were no other aftereffects from these encounters. There were no aggressive acts that took advantage of our loss of service. A similar type of electronic interference occurred in 2004. One of the Nimitz Carrier Group incidents involved a carrier-based fighter pilot who was unable to keep a weapons "lock" on a "tic tac" object shadowing his aircraft. Apparently, these objects can disable our weapons systems without permanently damaging them. While the motives for these actions are unknown, the pattern of disabling our weapons platforms have been a trait of this phenomenon for almost 70 years.

Congress will hopefully receive a report that gives some indication of what we are dealing with and recommendations on what Congress can do to address the phenomenon. However, given past history, cooperation with Congress will not be forthcoming. There are some steps that Congress can take to reassert its authority over service branches and agencies that receive funding from Congress. The Armed Services and Select Intelligence Committees can press the defense and intelligence communities for specifics about the "threat" that UFO/UAPs are to the United States and its allies. While it is apparent that the objects have superior technology, does this factor alone indicate a direct and imminent threat to the homeland? If there is evidence that these objects are manufactured and deployed by a terrestrial adversary, the threat is very real. Military advantages are not true advantages unless they are deployed. Recently declassified videos show, that except for observational incidents, these objects have not taken any aggressive steps against our fighter jets or ships in either carrier group (Nimitz & Roosevelt). Classified information may contradict this apparent lack of aggression. However, the public history of the phenomenon (pre-2004) does not indicate aggressive actions except those aimed at temporarily disabling our nuclear capabilities or weapons systems.

The four congressional committees must perform normal oversight to learn what information the military and intelligence communities possess about the phenomenon. Testimony of Nimitz Carrier Group personnel demonstrates that all electronic data was removed immediately after the incident. Congress needs to learn from the electronic records taken from the Nimitz Carrier Group. Congress should also call witnesses from the personnel who experienced these incidents to determine what happened. In either a classified or declassified setting, the 117th Congress should break its hands-off tradition and serve its normal oversight role.

If the Armed Services and Select Intelligence Committees do not get information that indicates a terrestrial adversary is the source of these objects, they will need to seek more information about the historical record of UFO/UAP contacts and how they impact the defense of the United States. The impact of a long-term phenomenon cannot be assessed based on three videos taken in 2004 and 2015. Since these videos are consistent with other accounts dating back to World War II, a review of other incidents and their impact on the military should be undertaken in both open and closed sessions. Open session is necessary to assure the American people that its elected representatives are taking this issue seriously after decades of official "debunking." Classified testimony will also be necessary to be able to understand the nature and magnitude of the potential threat without compromising national security.

If the defense and intelligence communities are not forthcoming about the issue for some reason, there are other methods at the disposal of Congress to learn the truth. Legislative changes that allow former military personnel to come forward and present Congress or an agency inspector general with their experiences can be adopted. Time limitations on security oaths, particularly for current or retired service personnel who were not part of a classified program, would allow them to provide information to Congress. Use of each agency's existing whistleblower programs could be an outlet for those who can speak about the findings of clandestine programs relevant to this inquiry.

Finally, if there is no plausible terrestrial source of the UFO/UAP phenomenon, Congress will need to coordinate our response with our allies and, possibly, our adversaries. A non-terrestrial source would likely not respond to a single country that holds four percent of the world's population. Even if the possibility of a non-terrestrial threat is real, unilateral actions will likely be counterproductive. Also, continued secrecy in the face of such a threat will harm any attempts at collective action. The past 70-plus years of secrecy has not brought us any closer to resolving this dilemma. The American people have a right to be informed of the true facts and to have their elected representatives set a proper policy course on their behalf.

II

SENATE SELECT INTELLIGENCE COMMITTEE
REFERRAL AND THE 117TH CONGRESS

THE 117TH CONGRESS WILL face many challenges. A contested presidential transition, the continuing COVID crisis, racial justice, economic issues, climate change, and other yet-to-be-foreseen issues. One of those challenges will soon be the response to the report requested by the Senate Select Intelligence Committee regarding unidentified anomalous phenomenon (UAP) being reviewed by the Navy's UAP Task Force. The purpose of this briefing book is to provide some background and context that may not be available to members of Congress from their defense and intelligence briefings.

On June 8, 2020, Senate Select Intelligence Committee Acting Chair Marco Rubio added language to the committee comments for Senate Bill 3095 (FY 2021 Intelligence Authorization Bill). The language requested the Director of National Intelligence (DNI) and the Secretary of Defense (SecDef) to coordinate activities to deal with a potential threat to our national security. In the short-term, it could help determine if another country has achieved a massive technological breakthrough that has put the United States at a severe disadvantage.

If no terrestrial breakthrough has been achieved, the long-term consequences could reveal one of the most important issues to face humanity.

The Senate Intel Committee's consensus request asked the defense and intelligence communities for a report about coordination in the study of UFO/UAPs. This is the first officially known effort to study recent military UFO/UAP sightings. Based on past experience and the tenor of its language, the direction of the request is reasonable in the short-term but raises long-term concerns. The referral is couched in terms of the "threat" these unknown objects pose to the defense of the United States. However, before this phenomenon is considered a threat to the United States, Congress must be apprised of the full set of facts about a subject that has been shrouded in mystery for at least 75 years.

The committee comment language requires the report be submitted to the four congressional armed services and intelligence committees within 180 days of the adoption of the Consolidated Appropriations Act, 2021.[2] The report is due to Congress on June 25, 2021. The request has two purposes, (1) to standardize UAP reporting procedures (Office of Naval Intelligence) and (2) to establish information sharing and coordination across agency boundaries (DNI consulting with the SecDef). For the first purpose, standardization includes "collection and reporting on unidentified aerial phenomenon, any links they have to adversarial foreign governments, and the threat they pose to U.S. military assets and installations." Much of the request is directed at information held by the Office of Naval Intelligence.

The standardization of UAP reporting, data collection, and analysis is recommended to be accomplished by the Office of Naval Intelligence, the current location of the UAP Task Force. The Senate Select Intelligence Committee "supports" their efforts. It appears to be

---

2   The Senate's version of the Intelligence Authorization Bill (S. 3905) was combined with the House version. The combined version was adopted as part of the combined COVID relief package and the funding of federal government for fiscal year 2021. (Consolidated Appropriations Act of 2021, Division W—Intelligence Authorization Act for Fiscal Year 2021.) By its terms under Section 3 of Division W, the consolidated bill incorporates the request of Senator Marco Rubio (R-Fla.) which contained the direction for the UAP report.

the Navy that is leading the effort to identify the UFO/UAPs. This request follows briefings given to certain committees that were prompted by Navy concerns over unknown objects near the Roosevelt (2014 & 2015) and Nimitz (2004) Carrier Groups. Gun camera footage of these objects has been circulating for several years. They received national attention after a December 16, 2017 *New York Times* article about the videos.[3] Since then, there have been more articles and many witnesses to these sightings that have come forward.

After some confusion in early 2020, the Pentagon confirmed that the videos were legitimate and declassified fuzzy versions. Two months earlier, the Defense Department had denied public access to these videos and, in one denial of a Freedom of Information Act (FOIA) request, stated that release of these videos would cause "grave danger to national security."[4] A significant policy reversal within two months. With the confirmation, the media exposure of this subject has substantially increased.

The Senate Intelligence Committee's request was also to establish protocols for information sharing across jurisdictional boundaries within the defense and intelligence communities. The specific language setting up the process is as follows:

> "Therefore, the Committee directs the DNI, in consultation with the Secretary of Defense and the heads of such other agencies as the Director and Secretary jointly consider relevant, to submit a report within 180 days of the date of enactment of the Act, to the congressional intelligence and armed services committees on unidentified aerial phenomena (also known as "anomalous aerial vehicles"), including observed airborne objects that have not been identified."

---

3   https://www.nytimes.com/2017/12/16/us/politics/unidentified-flying-object-navy.html
4   https://americanmilitarynews.com/2020/01/
      navy-says-secret-ufo-files-would-cause-grave-damage-to-us-national-security-if-released/

The primary responsibility is placed on the DNI.[5] The DNI is to "consult" with the SecDef. This consultation should include the heads of other agencies that they believe are relevant. The additional consulting agencies will primarily come from the 18 agencies under the authority of the DNI. Besides the Navy, the other branches of the Defense Department will likely be included. Outside of the defense and intelligence communities, NASA may also be asked to participate. One other possibility is the FBI, which is specifically mentioned in the comments. The Senate Intelligence Committee's committee comments specifically request that the FBI be consulted for intrusions into restricted U.S. airspace.

The Senate Intel Committee specifies what it wants included in the report. These items are requested using mandatory language ("directed"). This indicates the specific interests that the committee wants for a legitimate legislative purpose. In other words, the type of information intended to help the four congressional committees to craft future legislation. It lists eight categories of information which will be discussed in more detail in the next section.

The report needs to describe the process for coordination "ensuring timely data collection and centralized analysis of all unidentified aerial phenomena reporting for the federal government, regardless of which service or agency acquired the information." This requires each agency to follow a process that goes across agency boundaries, both military and civilian. A responsible official must be designated who is required to coordinate with other agencies. The committee has requested this specific information so that it can determine who is responsible for implementing the UAP policies at each agency. Lack of information and accountability has been a hallmark of the federal response to UFO/UAP issues that has stymied Congress for decades. Congressional

---

5   In August 2020, the Pentagon announced the appointment of Deputy Secretary of Defense David Norquist to oversee the Navy's UAP Task Force. This confused the lines of authority requested by the Senate Select Intelligence Committee. However, with the change in administrations, this briefing book will assume that the new administration will follow the original request of the Senate Intel Committee.

inquiries over the years have had little information about who handles the issues related to the UFO/UAP phenomenon. This requirement could allow for more accountability in the future.

The report to the four congressional committees requires "…(i)dentification of potential aerospace or other threats posed by the unidentified aerial phenomena to national security, and an assessment of whether this unidentified aerial phenomena activity may be attributed to one or more foreign adversaries." This requirement gets to the heart of the congressional inquiry. The report is to identify what threats are posed by UFO/UAPs. The details of the response to this item will likely be classified. As with any threat to the country, the first step would be for a classified analysis before any public disclosure. If the threat is attributed to a specific terrestrial adversary, it is also highly unlikely that it will be discussed in the public portion of the report.

The report requires the defense and intelligence communities to discuss "incidents or patterns that indicate a potential adversary may have achieved breakthrough aerospace capabilities that could put United States strategic or conventional forces at risk." This is aimed at terrestrial adversaries who have made a technological leap that puts our military forces at a severe disadvantage. Application of these factors to extraterrestrial visitation shows *a priori* that "they" meet both criteria as (1) a "potential adversary" and (2) that "they" have "achieved breakthrough aerospace capabilities." Without having achieved a technological breakthrough, they would not be here. It is unlikely that the report will jump to the conclusion that alien races are visiting Earth. To do so would require an explanation as to why Congress was just hearing about it. In addition, such explosive information would not be conveyed so quickly when official policy of the military and intelligence communities for 70-plus years is that all UFO/UAP claims are made by people who are (1) mistaken, (2) hoaxing, or (3) delusional. At best, the report, in its classified section, will leave breadcrumbs towards this possibility without throwing their own agencies under the collective "bus" for their past conduct.

Finally, the Intelligence Committee asks for recommendations about ways to study the phenomenon including funding needs. This final request ties the inquiry to a legislative purpose. In other words, give us your recommendations of how we can legislate new programs, including costs, to come up with answers to solve this mystery. The UAP language in the Senate Intel Committee comments is asking the entire defense and intelligence establishment to give the Intelligence and Armed Services Committees a legislative roadmap towards figuring this out. This places those who may have hidden the UFO/UAP phenomenon in charge of how, or if, disclosure will take place. Thus we are faced with a dilemma. Can the agencies that may have helped cover up this phenomenon be trusted to turn over a new leaf?

This document is intended to give the four congressional committees perspective and historical context to the information contained in the report, including the report's classified attachment. It is not an attempt to convince you that the UFO/UAP phenomenon proves there is an extraterrestrial presence on our planet. This briefing book discusses some of the history of the UFO/UAP phenomenon to educate you on past efforts that raise the same issues and concerns as today's disclosure of the three declassified videos that brought this issue to Congress.

A further purpose of these briefing materials is to give you background information to help you raise appropriate questions about the information presented to Congress in both public and closed sessions. This subject is fraught with misinformation in a culture where it is mostly consumed for entertainment purposes. The subject differs from most issues addressed by federal legislators. There are think tanks, academic institutions, special interest groups, and others who constantly supply Congress with information. Here, the only information that you will receive is from the defense and intelligence communities. While these sources are normally reliable, they have controlled this topic in the classified, compartmentalized world since World War II. During this period, public policy has been consistent. Official government policy is that this phenomenon does not exist. People who witness UFO/UAPs are either lying, delusional or simply mistaken. Yet, there are instances where a small number of sightings are unexplainable. Over time, the better our detection capabilities, the more unexplainable evidence is accumulated by our service branches and intelligence assets.

One assumption in the Senate Intel Committee's request is the possibility that this phenomenon poses a threat to the defense of the United States. There is a legitimate concern that another country might have achieved a technological breakthrough that, given the apparent capabilities of these unknown craft, would pose an existential threat to our security. Inquiries into this possibility are both necessary and appropriate. Actual evidence that a foreign country has achieved this kind of technological advance should be taken very seriously. If there is evidence of the existence of a successful program using advanced technology in another country, Congress would be remiss in its duties if it ignored this evidence.

Yet, if there is no evidence of a terrestrial source of these Navy sightings, a more nuanced approach may be in order. Absent a demonstrated terrestrial threat, the public policy review may include diplomatic issues and a broader global perspective to consider the implications of contact. However, much of this early process will depend on what constitutes a threat. The committee comments do not define the meaning of the term "threat." Without further direction from Congress, the military/intelligence community will define what constitutes a threat. This leaves broad discretion in unelected hands. By the time the report is issued, the four congressional committees will be predisposed to see the UFO/UAP phenomenon through a "threat response only" prism. To the detriment of the public, the threat angle will help keep matters in a classified setting, even in the absence of specific evidence of threatening conduct.

How the report addresses the "threat" premise will guide where this process leads. If the "threat" requires only proof of the existence of far superior technology to the United States military, one can see headlines that state, "Secret Defense Department Report Finds U.S. Under Threat by Unknown Technology: Seeks Funding to Address It." Once the phenomenon is seen as primarily a threat, there will be little public acknowledgement of the specifics of how the government is dealing with this "crisis." While there is a possibility that some UFO/UAPs are the product of a foreign terrestrial government, the public declaration of an "unknown threat" will likely brand the phenomenon as an ominous "military first" problem. As a hammer sees everything else as a "nail" to be pounded, the problem will be defined from a position of aggression rather than first trying to understand what we are dealing with.

However, if Congress can require proof of actual adverse activity instead of mere observation of our facilities, the branding of the "problem" will change from a "threat first" perspective to one that will allow for a more nuanced policy discussion. If the military/intelligence communities conclude there is a threat, the report, in the classified attachment, should have recent examples of UFO/UAPs doing more than just invading restricted airspace for observation purposes. Specific examples of aggressive actions should be required to demonstrate an actual threat. Without specific hostile acts showing evidence of bad intent, non-aggressive intrusions that amount to surveillance of our capabilities may not be considered a hostile intent without more information about the source of these objects.

If the report attributes these intrusions to terrestrial adversaries, they should be of concern because it is more likely we will be attacked by our own species. This kind of evidence would show that a hostile power has made a great leap in technology. Without specific evidence, the report will have problems attributing the threat to a specific terrestrial power. Doing so would focus attention on that country and may lead to a high-profile response from the country we accuse. If incorrect, such an accusation could do grave damage to the United States in the international arena. This possibility of using a foreign power as a scapegoat, without specific evidence, has too many risks for the military/intelligence communities and our diplomatic relations with the country at issue. However, if these intrusions cannot be attributed to a terrestrial source in the report, the issue will become much more complicated and likely hidden from the public while we "figure it out." If the report signals a vague allusion to a threat without documented aggressive acts, it will signal a "business as usual" attitude. The UFO/UAP phenomenon will remain a black program(s) with little or no information reaching the halls of Congress.

It is important the four committees learn the history of the UFO/UAP phenomenon as it relates to Congress' constitutional responsibilities of oversight. Given enough information, the committees will likely determine that the phenomenon is not a purely military/intelligence issue. Yet, given past history, the most likely result of the report will be a narrow focus on the terrestrial threat potential. It is likely that the terrestrial option will not be discarded even if there is no evidence to support it. Congress must be aware of the possibility that they will be given only vague information about the origins of this phenomenon as a general "fig leaf" to delay the inevitable disclosure of the true source of this mystery.

III

SENATE 3095: EIGHT REQUESTS ABOUT UNIDENTIFIED ANOMALOUS PHENOMENON

ON JUNE 8, 2020, Senator Marco Rubio (R-Florida) added language to the committee comments that were attached to the Intelligence Authorization Act for Fiscal Year 2021. (S. 3095 (116th Congress.)) The comments requested the Defense and Intelligence communities for a report about coordination efforts to study unidentified anomalous phenomenon (UAP), formerly UFOs (UFO/UAP). This is the first legislative step in response to the Navy's study of UFO/UAP sightings. It follows the April 2020 declassification of the videos taken in 2004 and 2015. In May 2020, the Pentagon acknowledged the existence of the UAP Task Force operating in the Office of Naval Intelligence (ONI). Based on past experience and the tenor of its language, the direction of the request is reasonable in the short-term but raises long-term concerns. The referral is couched only in terms of the "threat" these unknown objects pose to the defense of the United States. The request also has a narrow focus that could prevent Congress from addressing broader concerns that were raised when the report was requested. At a minimum, follow-up actions will be needed to give a more accurate picture of the phenomenon, especially the legitimate concerns of a technological breakthrough by a terrestrial adversary.

The committee comment language requires a report be submitted to the four congressional armed services and intelligence committees within 180 days of the adoption of the Consolidated Appropriations Act, 2021 (House Resolution No. 133, 116th Congress). The committee comments about UFO/UAPs have two policy purposes: (1) to standardize UAP reporting procedures (Office of Naval Intelligence) and (2) to establish information sharing and coordination across agency boundaries (Director of National Intelligence consulting with the Secretary of Defense). The request also asked for recommendations from the Director of National Intelligence and the Secretary of Defense. For the first purpose, standardization includes "collection and reporting on unidentified aerial phenomenon, any links they have to adversarial foreign governments, and the threat they pose to U.S. military assets and installations." While the language was not in the text of the bill, it was activated by passage of the annual authorization for the intelligence community for fiscal year 2021.[6] Each of the eight requests is discussed herein.

> (1) A detailed analysis of unidentified aerial phenomena data and intelligence reporting collected or held by the Office of Naval Intelligence, including data and intelligence reporting held by the Unidentified Aerial Phenomena Task Force.

At present, there is no uniform method for the United States government to gather and assess information about UFO/UAPs. Compartmentalized programs across the service branches and civilian

---

6   The Senate's version of the Intelligence Authorization Bill was subsumed within the House version. This version was adopted as part of the combined COVID relief package and the funding of federal government for fiscal year 2021. (Consolidated Appropriations Act of 2021, Division W—Intelligence Authorization Act for Fiscal Year 2021.) By its terms under Section 3 of Division W, the consolidated bill incorporates the report of Senator Marco Rubio (R-Fla.) which contained the direction for the UAP report. This report's deadline is 180 days from the approval of the Consolidated Appropriations Act of 2021. It is due on June 25, 2021.

intelligence agencies hinder the sharing of information. Much like the intelligence failures pre-911, the protection of the country is hampered by divisions between service branches, intelligence agencies, and law enforcement. The possibility that China, Russia or another terrestrial foreign power has achieved a massive technological breakthrough could be hidden from view. The government may possess segments of the overall intelligence picture behind classified bureaucratic walls. In making its referral, the consensus of the Senate Intel Committee indicated that they favor the intelligence gathering approach taken by the Office of Naval Intelligence. What that approach entails is not publicly known. The Intel Committee did not request similar information from other agencies or service branches to compare with the Navy's approach. No historical information about how information collection and analysis of UFO/UAPs was requested.

Missing from the request is any reference to the intelligence gathering approach of the Air Force or the newly formed Space Force to the UFO/UAP phenomenon. The DNI, after consulting with the SecDef, would have to decide to include Air Force information. In the past, the Air Force had primary responsibility for gathering intelligence about UFO/UAPs. Also, the programs that were transferred to the Space Force would surely include detection and analysis of unknown objects in Earth orbit or potential Earth-based sources of the phenomenon. Each of the four committees receiving the requested report could surely learn lessons from the procedures established by these two service branches and other agencies, both in the past and as they function today.

While the consensus of the Senate Intel Committee was that ONI has the proper approach, ONI does not have primary responsibility for unknown objects outside Earth's atmosphere. It also has limited global reach in that the Navy relies on other agencies to supply much of its real-time global intelligence. The past and present policies of Air Force Intelligence, Surveillance and Reconnaissance (25th Air Force), National Geospatial Intelligence Agency (NGA) and the National

Reconnaissance Office (NRO) are missing from this request. They will only be supplied if the DNI determines the congressional committees should have this information. It is left up to the DNI, in consultation with SecDef, to determine what agencies should be consulted in developing common policies and providing information to the Armed Services and Intel Committees. If comprehensive information from these other sources is not provided in the report, the report will only provide a partial picture to Congress. The past and present policies for collection and analysis of UFO/UAPs by the 25th Air Force, Space Force, NGA and NRO should also be reviewed. Forming a cooperative network must include all resources at the disposal of our government if this referral is to develop a comprehensive policy.

Inclusion of the NRO, NGA, Air and Space Force policies will help the four committees understand how other agencies with different responsibilities have handled UFO/UAP incidents. It is unlikely that the Navy policies will address the full range of capabilities of objects that might originate in another country. Of the three Naval videos declassified this year, each begins after the objects are already close to a Navy carrier group. However, the origin of these objects must still be determined to give the military a realistic chance to defend itself. Establishing protocols to react to craft with unique performance characteristics requires earlier warning systems and protocols. Learning about a threat once it is in range of our military assets will be too late. The entire range of our detection capabilities must be brought into play if these craft are indeed a terrestrial threat.

For instance, some of the 2004 Nimitz Carrier Group sightings started with radar target acquisition of dozens of objects heading south from Catalina and Coronado Islands, off the Southern California coast. However, they did not originate from these islands. They must have originated someplace else. How they got to these islands in the first place is still likely unknown. There are several terrestrial possibilities. First, they could have been launched from a foreign ship or submarine in the area. Another possibility is that they were launched from long-range foreign aircraft. A third possibility is that they flew from foreign soil. A fourth possibility is that they were launched from a space platform.

In each of these scenarios, the protocols developed by the Navy may not address information-sharing and analysis needed in real time to deal with the potential threat. Once spotted by the Navy, it will have little time to react. The protocols developed by ONI may not consider or may not mesh with the capabilities of the other agencies that view a broader area from a space-based perspective.

Just applying Naval protocols to other agencies may not address the source of these unknown threats. The committees should focus upon the terrestrial origins of these objects either before they reach our military assets or be able to track their movements back to their source. This will require the committees to have information about the policies of UFO/UAP tracking by other agencies with a space-based or otherwise global perspective. Just working off the Naval protocols will not achieve that goal.

For the purposes of the report due on June 25, 2021, this limitation on UFO/UAP data is necessary. The difficulty with compiling data in a short period justifies the limitation to Naval intelligence data. However, this limitation will give the congressional committees only a glimpse at the data and intelligence analysis done by other service branches and intelligence agencies. Most of the data is likely held within compartmentalized programs that do not share information with each other. Hence, there is a problem with lack of coordination. Another complication for Congress will be delays caused by the contested transition between presidential administrations.

It is likely that a response from ONI will be limited to sightings beginning with the November 2004 Nimitz Carrier Group incident. To date, only three incidents have been declassified, 2004 (FLIR.mp4), 2014 (Gimbal.wmv), and 2015 (GOFAST.wmv).[7] These three were

---

7   https://www.navair.navy.mil/foia/documents

recorded over open water off of the Atlantic and Pacific Oceans close to United States territorial waters. However, it is highly unlikely that the phenomenon is limited to offshore locations.

Another specific request is made to the Federal Bureau of Investigation (FBI) regarding land-based intrusions into restricted airspace within the United States. This narrow request for information may serve the initial purpose of providing information in a short period of time, but it fails to provide a full picture of congressional efforts to determine the source(s) of the UFO/UAP phenomenon. Assuming a terrestrial source for this phenomenon, overflights of domestic territory are as concerning as offshore incidents. Restricting the scope of information to the FBI and the Navy will leave gaps in coverage, making the establishment of new programs and policies potentially inadequate. Considering the potential threat to the homeland, if these objects are being seen over sensitive locations such as domestic Air Force, Marine, and Army bases, the limitations of the scope of the study will not reflect the true nature of the threat. Follow-up requests for data about domestic incursions will be necessary to understand the full scope of the UFO/UAP phenomenon.

(2) A detailed analysis of unidentified phenomena data collected by geospatial intelligence, signals intelligence, human intelligence, and measurement and signals intelligence.

The request of the Senate Intel Committee asks for information from various methods of data collection typically used by the intelligence community. Each of these methods is centered on intelligence gathering by the 18 intelligence agencies. Which agencies provide information is up to the DNI after consulting with the SecDef. The choice of which agency provides information is left in the hands of appointed officials and not Congress. Since the request is not actually part of the language of the Intelligence Authorization Act, the choice of which agencies comply with the request does not have the force of law. Nothing in the language of the Intel Committee request requires the DNI to provide data from any agency that the DNI, after consultation with the SecDef, determines should not present data to the Armed Services and Intel Committees. Partisan reasons or concerns over jurisdictional "turf" may lead to a narrowing of the sources of data provided to Congress. Since much of the data is contained in compartmentalized (need-to-know) programs, there is a strong probability that the report will only contain information that is in programs that the four congressional committees already know about. There is a strong likelihood information that would help Congress make informed decisions will be left out of the report.

This selective choice of data could be exacerbated by the transition between presidential administrations. The required level of cooperation between the outgoing DNI and SecDef and the incoming office-holders is not likely, given the current political climate. The incoming DNI and SecDef may not have the time or the knowledge of the existence of relevant programs that would help Congress in its oversight role. The Armed Services and Intel Committees need to question the appropriate officials to ensure that they have been provided with all the information that is necessary to complete an appropriate review of these matters. If there are programs that these committees do not have the appropriate clearance to review, subcommittees (*i.e.* Intelligence and Emerging Threats and Capabilities) can be used to review highly-classified data from programs the executive branch may be reluctant to release. Dividing up tasks among various subcommittees will decrease the number of people that need to be authorized to review highly-classified data. This option may be a compromise that allows Congress to learn about programs it needs to know about to perform its oversight functions.

"Human intelligence" data must also be provided. However, it is unclear whether this requires information from actual trained witnesses to these incidents. As shown in later sections, previous government studies of the UFO/UAP phenomenon have all suffered from the absence of actual firsthand witnesses. There is no request for the DNI or the SecDef to provide eyewitnesses to the incidents that gave rise to this inquiry. Typically, congressional hearings have testimony from administration officials who oversee the issues that are under review. In addition, Congress routinely hears from those who are directly affected by the issue or can provide firsthand testimony about the issue.

Here, in the case of the three Navy videos, there are multiple witnesses who can provide context to the photographic and radar evidence that should be part of the requested report. Eyewitness accounts of these three incidents and related unexplained phenomenon will help Congress understand how the military reacts to these incidents. Camera footage will not help Congress determine what kinds of training and other preparatory steps are needed to be ready to confront a new terrestrial threat. This testimony can be held in an open or closed setting depending on the situation. Of the three partially declassified incidents (2004–2015), most of the testimony could be conducted in public session since the footage is publicly available.

If the inquiry is to have the trust of the American people, actual witnesses will help this inquiry maintain its integrity. If the inquiry is limited to the three incidents with declassified video footage, the failure to hear from the actual witnesses will show a lack of curiosity that will undermine any congressional findings. Since all three declassified videos were taken by military personnel, the committees will have the ability to speak directly to trained observers such as pilots, radar operators, command officers, and regular sailors who viewed all or part of any incident. These direct witnesses can testify to their impressions as to how these highly unusual situations were handled in real time. They could suggest policies or procedures that could help military personnel react to these incidents in the future. Trained witness impressions may provide data that does not appear in videos or radar tapes which could provide clues to the origin of these objects. Without the human element, policies that are developed may not reflect actual conditions that are faced by our military personnel.

(3) A detailed analysis of data of the FBI, which was derived
from investigations of intrusions of unidentified aerial phenomena data over restricted United States airspace.

The specific referral to the FBI is surprising. Since September
1947, the Bureau has expressly denied any involvement with the UFO/
UAP phenomenon. The request covers all restricted airspace in the
United States. Yet, restricted airspace in the United States is regulated
or controlled by many agencies and service branches who were not
specifically asked to provide data. Restricted airspace includes coverage
of both civilian and military facilities. Each type of restricted airspace
is regulated by different agencies who are not requested to provide information. As applied to airspace above federal government facilities,
the FBI would be the logical choice. However, there are many other
areas of restricted airspace that are above facilities that fall under the
jurisdiction of other agencies.

The Federal Aviation Administration (FAA) has regulatory authority over civilian airports. These locations are of defense significance,
serving the logistical needs of the armed forces during conflicts. The
FAA has jurisdiction over air safety concerns and should have records
about air safety incidents with UFO/UAPs. The risk to passenger safety
and the threat to our ability to respond to an attack should be reviewed
by the Armed Services and Intel Committees. Gathering information
from the FAA would aid the investigation. If the source is a terrestrial
adversary, related civilian air safety data could be of assistance.

Similarly, the Department of Energy, Office of Intelligence and
Counterintelligence would be another non-military source of information about intrusions into restricted airspace above nuclear power
plants. It is unlikely that the FBI would have all restricted airspace
intrusion information that is possessed by the Department of Energy
(DOE). The contingency plans of the DOE for nuclear plant safety
should be of defense interest. As discussed in later sections, interest
of UFO/UAPs in our military nuclear facilities raise similar questions

about their interest in civilian nuclear facilities. Are UFO/UAPs interested only in military uses of nuclear power or are they also interested in civilian uses? Anecdotal evidence suggests both.

In addition to these objects' interest in nuclear assets, what other facilities attract their interest? It would be valuable to learn from each service branch about air intrusions over domestic military facilities. It is unlikely that the FBI would have data on violations of restricted airspace above Army, Marine, Air Force, or Coast Guard facilities. A broader net should be cast to see how these sensitive military installations have responded to UFO/UAP incursions.

Once again, the request for information from the FBI is important. However, this request is only part of the puzzle. Information on domestic restricted airspace violations by unknown flying objects is held in many other locations. If not provided in the report, the committees should ask for follow-up information before setting long-term uniform policies.

> (4) A detailed description of an interagency process for ensuring timely data collection and centralized analysis of all unidentified aerial phenomena reporting for the federal government, regardless of which service or agency acquired the information.

This request is important to determine if the agencies and service branches have established a process that allows cooperation in the short- and long-term. In the long-term, coordination will assist in establishing trends that will help determine the origin of these unknown craft. Data sharing will prevent duplication of effort and will help determine if there are gaps in the analysis. Only a holistic approach will help establish the terrestrial source of this phenomenon, if any.

In the short-term, until terrestrial sources are ruled out, there should be an urgency to establishing an interagency process. If a terrestrial source exists, the likelihood of an attack is heightened. A country

UFO BRIEFING BOOK

that possesses the ability to enter our airspace and surveil our military assets from close range has a significant advantage that will be very tempting to exploit. If these craft have weapons systems, the risk of their use is remarkably high. Military advances usually give a country a short-term advantage. Hence, the temptation is to use the advantage before others acquire it.

If there is evidence that one of our adversaries possesses a significant technological advantage, data collection and centralized analysis are only the first steps in the preparatory process. If there is classified evidence of a specific terrestrial source, preparation to defend against the threat should be a first priority.

(5) Identification of an official accountable for the process described in paragraph 4.

The naming of a responsible official in charge of UFO/UAP data collection and analysis for each responsible agency is a step forward. For decades, citizens who wanted access to unclassified documents about the phenomenon had trouble determining who was in charge of these efforts. Assuming the names and/or titles of these personnel are unclassified, the official accountable to the process will be known to the public. In addition, it is an important step for Congress that allows them to know whom to send requests for information about this subject. Accountability to the Congress and the public is a fundamental requirement for a democracy.

(6) Identification of potential aerospace or other threats posed by the unidentified aerial phenomena to national security, and an assessment of whether this unidentified aerial phenomena activity may be attributed to one or more foreign adversaries.

This request gets at the heart of the Senate Intel Committee's concerns. Have foreign adversaries achieved a technological break-through that puts the United States at a severe disadvantage in a future conflict? Were these unknown craft probing our defenses in 2004 when they were seen visually and on radar 100 miles off the coast of California? The answers to these questions are crucial to our national defense.

Using the 2004 Nimitz Carrier Group incidents as a starting point, the four congressional committees have a wealth of data to review. In addition to the gun camera footage, there are eyewitnesses and real time electronic data that can be reviewed by the Navy and presented as part of the report. These will help Congress understand the performance capabilities of these objects. Even from publicly revealed eyewitness accounts, there are many details that can be used by the DNI and SecDef to inform Congress. If this kind of detail is not contained in the report or its classified appendix, the four committees should hear from the witnesses and review the electronic records to see for themselves.

Some things are known about these objects. They move under their own power but have no visible means of propulsion. The infrared cameras did not pick up a heat signature from the objects, which would indicate a traditional power source. As discussed in Section V, the radar on the U.S.S. Princeton, an Aegis Cruiser, witnessed a drop in altitude from 80,000 to 20,000 feet in 0.75 seconds. The speed of this descent would kill a pilot flying high-performance aircraft from the sheer g-force. Also, in one instance after an engagement with one of these objects, the fighter jet returned to its patrol station, the unknown object was already at our pilot's combat air patrol (CAP) coordinates. This indicates foreknowledge of the classified CAP location.

Obviously, these craft, piloted or remote-controlled, have performance characteristics far beyond our most advanced aircraft. They also have the ability to anticipate our reactions instantaneously. With all of these abilities, they seem to avoid contact and do not appear to take a threatening posture. Observation may have been the motive for their actions.

If they are of terrestrial origin, why would they engage in this behavior? One possibility is that they are probing our defenses. Yet, assuming these craft are prototypes, why would an adversary test them so close to our borders? One does not test new craft near hostile forces. The chances of losing a craft and it being reverse engineered by an adversary would be too great. Because of the location, numbers, and their confident manner of engagement of the Nimitz Carrier Group, it is unlikely that they are prototypes still being tested. According to service personnel that witnessed the events, there were so many of these vehicles that a reasonable assumption is that they must already be in service. This possibility means that the determination of the terrestrial source is of critical importance. In determining the source, the committees need to look for evidence of how the objects got 100 miles off of the Southern California coast and how they returned to their point of origin. Since the objects first appeared near Catalina and the Coronado Islands, they were probably registering on radar of civilian and military bases from Vandenburg Air Force Base to Coronado Naval Air Station. In addition, satellite coverage is a possibility. These avenues should have been explored by the military and/or intelligence community, considering the seriousness of the intrusion. Each committee should request the data from these sources to help understand the location of the terrestrial source.

The Nimitz Carrier Group incidents were in November 2004. Assuming a terrestrial adversary had this operational technology 16 years ago, other data should be available to the committees of other incidents. If the objects are of terrestrial origin, there could be better glimpses of these objects through newer technical means by 2021. These intrusions should be studied for signs of hostile intent. The DNI and SecDef should have a significant amount of data drawn from national technical means, human intelligence, and eyewitness reports even assuming that the 2004 incident was the first terrestrial incursion into areas where we had Naval assets. The Air Force should have similar data since these objects are airborne and are likely not limited to flight above bodies of water. Data from geospatial and other Earth orbit surveillance methods should help track these unknown objects either from their terrestrial sources or back to their place of origin.

(7) Identification of any incidents or patterns that indicate a potential adversary may have achieved breakthrough aerospace capabilities that could put United States strategic or conventional forces at risk.

As discussed above, the necessity of tracking these objects to their place of origin is of critical importance to protect the country's military assets. Without knowledge of the terrestrial source, it will be difficult to plan counter measures. Assuming Defense Department concern started in 2004 with the first of the unclassified incidents, there has been 16 years to gather information about this potential threat. The potential consequences of a terrestrial adversary with a fleet of craft that cannot be tracked through infrared heat signatures and have performance characteristics considered impossible by current science should be cause for alarm. In one respect, the 180 day timeline is short for a response. On the other hand, the DNI and SecDef represent agencies and service branches that have had at least 16 years to prepare for this eventuality.

The only question about the report contents should be what information should be in the report and what portions should be in the classified appendix. Refusal to share the information should not be an option to the Article I branch of government that controls the purse strings. Any concerns over briefing so many members of Congress about the details of specific classified programs should not prevent a briefing of smaller subcommittees with appropriate jurisdiction. The request of the Select Senate Intelligence Committee included a request for information on funding and other legislative fixes. Congress cannot accurately assess the needs of the intelligence community and service branches without this information.

Taking the word of these agencies and service branches without specific information should not be an option. The potential threat of a terrestrial adversary that has been known to exist for at least 16 years. If the necessary information about evidence as to the potential source is not presented, it will indicate several possible problems. First, the DNI and SecDef are unwilling to advise Congress on the results of programs studying the phenomenon despite the fact these programs were paid for through congressional appropriations. Such a refusal should indicate that the executive departments are undeserving of funding for this issue. Further inquiries should be mandatory to preserve our system of checks and balances. Second, there might be no information that points to a terrestrial source of this phenomenon. This would mean other alternatives must be investigated. Third, the DNI and SecDef are unwilling to admit a lack of effort that could be the equivalent of a Pearl Harbor or 911 failure of intelligence. If a "game-changing" advantage is held by one of our adversaries, there is a heightened chance that they will use it in the near future before the advantage is lost. Consider the aggressive military actions our main adversaries (China and Russia) are taking during a pandemic. The Ukraine, Syria, South China Sea, and Kashmir are just a few examples. Military secrets are the most fleeting and are eventually exposed. An advantage is not an advantage unless it is used. Finally, it is also possible that the military is aware that the phenomenon is not of terrestrial origin but has not informed Congress of its true nature.

Regardless of the reason, Congress should require specific background information about the necessity of any funding request before approving new appropriations. Regardless of the source of these objects, potential responses should not be left to appointed administrative personnel. Some basic level of understanding of the nature and source of any potential threat should be a baseline for Congress to consider legislative steps and funding. As discussed below, many past excesses by the defense and intelligence agencies have been the result, in part, of the Congress neglecting its oversight role.[8]

(8) Recommendations regarding increased collection of data, enhanced research and development, and additional funding and other resources.

Recommendations for funding and legislation must have support of a factual record. Evidence of an actual terrestrial threat should be necessary to support any request for legislation and appropriations. At present, the public record merely shows a mystery without a nexus to link it to a foreign adversary. Without that link, funding and legislation should have a broader perspective and not be dealt with in a purely military context.

If legislation is proposed, it should be targeted towards the possibilities about the phenomenon rather than a preprogramed assumption that UAPs must be from a foreign adversary. The origins of the UFO/UAP mystery should be aimed at what we know that is actually shown to Congress, rather than based on assumptions of intelligence that is not shared with Congress. As the originator of all federal funding, Congress should only act on what can be shown in testimony and evidence presented in open or closed hearings.

Any legislation should be controlling and not contradicted by previous executive directives or legislation. Any bill establishing a program or new funding should be clear that it supersedes any previous laws, orders, rules, or regulations. The legislation must include language that, "notwithstanding" any other previous guidance on this subject, this legislation supersedes any previous act, order, or legislation. This way the Congress will set new policy going forward.

Legislative findings should also be attached to new legislation and

---

8   Church Committee (U.S. Senate Select Committee on Intelligence Activities Within the United States), "Intelligence Activities and the Rights of Americans: 1976 U.S. Senate Report on Illegal Wiretaps and Domestic Spying by the FBI, CIA and NSA", Red and Black Publishers (2007).

appropriations. These findings should be based on the entirety of the federal record on this subject, not just what was cherrypicked to advocate a bureaucratic imperative. It should reference information that should be presented to Congress about pre-2004 incidents and not limited to evidence that has recently caught public attention. As discussed herein, this is necessary because of the Defense Department's pattern of focusing on each UFO/UAP incident in isolation rather than trying to understand overall trends. Finally, the American people should be informed of what is being done to address this issue. As will be shown, there is a history of policy in this area of clandestine programs being conducted without the knowledge of the four committees. It is critical that the Congress conduct true oversight of this issue and make as much information as possible available to the American people.

IV

HISTORICAL ANALYSIS OF FEDERAL GOVERNMENT UFO/UAP INVOLVEMENT

WHEN IT COMES TO UFO/UAPs, the United States has been repeating the same pattern for over 75 years. Mysterious cases that defy simple answers are treated as a public relations problem. For cases with strong evidence that cannot be easily discounted, there is confusion and fumbled attempts to determine a cause that fits into an official, pre-established narrative. The techniques used to determine a cause are seldom designed to explore firsthand evidence. For those cases that cannot be categorized as misidentification, the officials cast doubt on the motives or sanity of the witnesses. Cases that had a tenuous explanation were considered as "identified," no matter how farfetched the explanation. Officials always assumed that there is no evidence of a potential nonterrestrial cause despite being unable to explain data that contradicts this assumption. After each go-around, the official policy remains the same. Every single sighting is the result of (1) mistaken identity, (2) deliberate deception, or (3) the product of a delusional mind. Eventually, the public turns the page when another issue grabs the headlines. Later, another triggering incident starts the process anew.

Today, we are in the same place we were in the 1940s. A question mark with no final answer. Yet, the 1942–1945 phenomenon experienced by Army Air Corp pilots differs little from what has been captured on three declassified videos from 2004 to 2015. This section discusses the similarities between the government's response to past events and today's conundrum. In many respects, the only differences between World War II "foo fighters" and the Nimitz "tic tacs" are today's better cameras and radar.

Whether this cycle is by design or the product of poor investigative techniques, the same mistakes have been repeated over the modern era of the UFO/UAP phenomenon. Investigations are done in a haphazard manner. Normal investigatory procedures are not followed. Untrained local Air Force officers investigated cases and forwarded reports to a central location. The cause of most cases was resolved by personnel who never left Wright-Patterson Air Force Base. This raises questions about the results and the government's intention to even understand the phenomenon.[9] A separate classified system for military sightings existed and the analysis of these cases has not been made public. As a result, the public's confidence in each outcome is lacking. Polling of American opinion shows a significant lack of trust in the government's intentions to address this phenomenon.[10]

Congress has attempted to hold substantive hearings on the UFO/UAP phenomenon over the years.[11] Save for one short hearing on July 29, 1968[12], congressional efforts have been limited to cryptic Air Force briefings or outright refusals to participate in open congressional oversight hearings. This administrative pushback has been non-partisan. Party leaders such as House Majority Leader John McCormick and

---

9   Hynek, J. Allen, The UFO Experience: A Scientific Inquiry, Henry Regnery Company, (1972), Appendix 4 (Excerpt of a letter from J. Allen Hynek to Colonel Raymond S. Sleeper), pp. 251.

10   YouGov poll, June 26, 2020, 56% of Americans believe that the United States Government would hide information about UFO/UAPs. https://today.yougov.com/topics/science/articles-reports/2020/07/07/us-government-ufos-aliens-poll-data.

11   Jacobs, David, UFO Controversy in America, Signet Books (1975), pp. 140–170.

12   Hearings Before the House Committee on Science and Aeronautics (90th Congress, Second Session), Symposium on Unidentified Flying Objects, July 29, 1968.

House Minority Leader Gerald Ford are among those who advocated oversight hearings.

This section reviews some, but not all, of these efforts. One common theme over a 75 year period is minimal congressional involvement. The normal oversight functions of the people's representatives have been missing in action. Whether these objects are new or have been around for a significant period is unknown because, in part, of the way that Congress has maintained a mostly hands-off approach. When sincere interest in understanding the source of the few, highly credible cases, the Air Force was able to outmaneuver or limit the scope of these efforts. Those in Congress who have attempted to understand this mystery have been unable to break this cycle. If the four congressional committees are going to play a role, a new approach needs to be taken that uses normal oversight methods which assure the public a genuine attempt is being made to understand the phenomenon.

Foo Fighters (1942–1945)

During both the European and Pacific campaigns, Army Air Corp pilots were shadowed by balls of light (small orbs) and other objects with no visible means of propulsion, mostly over hostile territory. While there were some differences between the two theaters of operation, both had bright orbs during night flights and other strangely-shaped daytime objects that were generally known as "foo fighters." The name was taken from the comic strips, but the phenomenon was real. These objects bore a remarkable resemblance to the objects in the recently declassified aerial footage, particularly the Roosevelt GOFAST.wmv video. Based on publicly available information, no definitive answers about foo fighters were ever determined by the military.

A typical sighting was during a bombing mission, over enemy territory. Either the bombers or their escorts would be shadowed by lighted orbs. Some saw more traditional "flying saucers." However, most were small with variations over time and geography. Formations of planes would have these balls of light off their wings which shadowed the formation. They mimicked the movements of our aircraft for long distances. When gunners would fire at the objects, they seemed unaffected.

Ball lightening and St. Elmo's Fire were considered likely suspects but neither matched the testimony of pilots or the weather conditions. While the Allies were puzzling over the cause of the objects, so were Germany and Japan. Each side assumed they were a secret weapon of the other side. A *New York Times* front page story, on January 2, 1945, discussed the mystery.[13]

While there are only a few declassified, cryptic flight notes about them, there is little available information about military efforts to determine a cause. What is known is that the U.S. military had several scientists look into them. Geophysicist David Griggs was considered by colleagues as the most knowledgeable about the phenomenon. He was a civilian scientist that worked for the Office of the Secretary of War during World War II. He later served as the Chief Scientist for the Air Force (1951–1952). Griggs reviewed Japanese war records after the war and could not find any ties to Japanese technology.[14] Griggs concluded that many of the foo fighters were true unknowns.[15] Physicists Harold Percy Robertson (CalTech) and Luis Alvarez (University of California (Berkeley)) also studied the foo fighter phenomenon for the military. No report of their conclusions is available to the public.

There are many common traits between today's public information about military sightings and the accounts of foo fighters. No terrestrial cause was found for foo fighters or for today's phenomenon. Weather phenomena was considered and rejected as they were seen during all types of weather. They came close to our aircraft but did not exhibit any hostile intent. They would mimic the maneuvers of our aircraft. If any reason for their presence could be detected, it was merely

---

13 https://timesmachine.nytimes.com/timesmachine/1945/01/02/issue.html
14 Swords, Michael, D.; Powell, Robert, UFOs and Government: A Historical Inquiry, Anomalist Books (2012), pp. 3–7.
15 Id @ pp. 7.

observation. While there are photographs of the objects, none have the picture quality of the current unclassified footage.

Little is known about the results of the Army Air Corp investigation efforts. There is no report showing the results of any formal investigation. There are only excerpts in Army Air Corps unit reports and vague press reports that merely speculate as to their origin. Since there is no real paper trail of the military efforts to find a cause, we have little information to determine what these investigations actually found. Later investigations merely make references to the fact the foo fighter phenomenon existed, but there is no concrete information to help future investigations that put the sightings in a broader context. Later reviews of the same subject have largely ignored whatever efforts were put into the study of the World War II foo fighters.

THE FLYING SAUCER WAVE AND ITS AFTERMATH (1947–1954)

During the summer of 1947, a flying saucer wave swept the nation. Kenneth Arnold, while searching for a plane crash in eastern Washington, saw nine objects that skipped through the air like a "saucer on water." While other sightings pre-dated the Arnold sighting, it was his sighting that captured the attention of the country. From July 4 to 9, 1947, discs were sighted in Washington, Oregon, Idaho, and California by pilots including two commercial, two Air Force, and one aviation magazine editor.[16] However, most of the early reports came from not so credible sources.

At first, there was no uniform policy for dealing with the effects of the phenomenon. Did the phenomenon pose a genuine threat to national security? If so, who was behind the threat? Had the Soviets made a giant technological leap? Were we testing secret weapons? Confusion reigned in the military and intelligence communities.

The newly-formed Air Force had difficulty coping with the

---

16   National Investigations Committee on Aerial Phenomenon (NICAP), Richard H. Hall (Editor), The UFO Evidence (1964), reprint Barnes & Noble Books (1997), pp. 33.

phenomenon. They assigned responsibility to the Air Technical Intelligence Center (ATIC) at Wright-Patterson Air Force Base (Wright Field until 1948) in Dayton, Ohio. They tried to investigate cases on an individual basis with a small staff. In 1947 there was a flood of reports and most had prosaic explanations. From 1947 through early 1949, the Air Force investigators eventually broke into two camps. Those in favor of the extraterrestrial hypothesis and those against. While there were some in the middle who thought that more data was needed, the period was marked by a struggle to figure it out.

Other explanations were considered and discarded. The Air Force denied that UFOs were a secret military program. They also discarded the idea that the phenomenon was of foreign terrestrial origin. Why would a foreign power test a new weapon over populated areas of another country? The risk of loss and the possibility that the technology would fall into the wrong hands was too great.

Several significant incidents kept the phenomenon from disappearing from the public eye even as the number of sightings dwindled after 1947. On January 7, 1948, a tragic crash occurred in Kentucky that changed many people's perspective about the phenomenon.[17] Fort Knox's Godman Field received a UFO report from the Kentucky Highway Patrol. Reports in the area were of a 300-foot-wide UFO flying near the base. An incoming flight of P-51 fighter planes (high-performance propeller-driven aircraft) were asked to investigate. The lead pilot, Captain Thomas Mantell, chased what he called, according to disputed accounts from the air traffic controllers, "an object of tremendous size." Having left the rest of his wing behind, Capt. Mantell chased the object to an altitude of 20,000 feet. An experienced combat pilot, Mantell did this without oxygen in a maneuver beyond recommended altitudes. During his chase of the object, his plane crashed, killing him, and leaving a mystery behind.

---

17   Ruppelt, Edward, J., The Report on Unidentified Flying Objects (Original 1956 Edition) Doubleday & Company, reissued Cosimo Classics (2011), pp. 31–34; Clark, Jerome, The UFO Book: Encyclopedia of the Extraterrestrial (1998), Visible Ink Press, pp. 351–356.

The Air Force first claimed he was chasing Venus in broad daylight. However, Venus was barely visible and would only be a pinprick of light that the observer would have to know where to look to even find. An alternative explanation was that a weather balloon was the object he was chasing. However, no balloon was in the area at the time. The Air Force went back and forth through various explanations, but none matched the facts. This was the first publicly acknowledged fatality involving a "flying saucer."

After the 1947 wave, the number of sightings declined. However, the quality of the sightings improved.[18] A higher percentage of the 1948 and 1949 sightings were by credible observers. Military and civilian pilots, law enforcement, scientists and other trained observers were giving detailed accounts that could not be easily dismissed as "mass hysteria" or "war nerves."[19] Airline pilots, military officers, and public safety personnel, trained in observational skills, were speaking to the press about their sightings.

One significant example that captured the public's imagination was a sighting by two airline pilots and a passenger that raised airline safety questions. On July 24, 1948, an Eastern Airlines flight was flying near Montgomery, Alabama. Pilot Clarence Chiles and copilot Charles Whitted were at an altitude of 5,000 feet, preparing to land.

An unknown object appeared in the distance. As the object got closer, they noticed that it was shaped like the fuselage of a passenger plane without wings or a tail. The craft had two rows of windows and the bottom glowed blue. It had orangish flames coming out of the back. The object came within a half a mile while they were on their landing approach in restricted airspace. The pilots estimated that the object was about 500 feet higher than their position when it streaked past their DC-6, four-engine propeller-driven aircraft. While most passengers

---

18   Ruppelt, Edward, J., The Report on Unidentified Flying Objects (Original 1956 Edition) Doubleday & Company, reissued Cosimo Classics (2011); kevinrandle.blogspot.com/2018/07/donald-keyhoe-and-thomas-mantell.html (Major Donald Keyhoe perspective).
19   Ruppelt, Edward, J., The Report on Unidentified Flying Objects (Original 1956 Edition) Doubleday & Company, reissued Cosimo Classics (2011).

were asleep at the time, one passenger, a respected business executive, saw a blue streak go by the plane, confirming the pilots' description.[20]

As with the Mantell incident, air safety issues were raised. The DC-6 was on landing approach and the unknown object made a close pass in restricted airspace. The sighting came at a time when the Air Force was trying to reassure the public that the phenomenon was not a threat. The incident fanned the flames of public interest when reported sightings were on the wane. It seemed that, just when the Air Force thought it was over the hump, the phenomenon would reappear and raise new concerns.

Air Force Captain Edward J. Ruppelt, Senior Officer for the Air Force's Project Blue Book, commented that the Mantell crash and the Chiles/Whitted sighting created quite a stir among the Project Sign, a predecessor program to Blue Book, personnel at ATIC. Both incidents breathed new life into the extraterrestrial hypothesis.

According to Captain Ruppelt and Major Dewey J. Fournet, Jr., an Air Force "Estimate of the Situation" was prepared including discussion of the possibility of extraterrestrial visitation. The Estimate was sent up the chain of command. When it reached Air Force Chief of Staff Hoyt S. Vandenberg, he rejected its conclusions and ordered all copies destroyed.

The rejection of this memorandum indicated to ATIC that senior brass discouraged any discussion of the extraterrestrial hypothesis. It was considered a turning point and, while there were many high-quality unexplained sightings at the time, the official Air Force policy no longer considered extraterrestrial visitation as a possible option.

In 1952 when Captain Ruppelt took over Project Blue Book, he organized flying saucer reports from 1947 onward. There had been no real organized analysis of the sightings that were reported to the Air Force. There was no organized filing system that could be used to detect patterns. Ruppelt documented a decrease in sightings, during

---

20 Clark, Jerome, The UFO Book: Encyclopedia of the Extraterrestrial (1998), Visible Ink Press, pp. 33–35.

1948–1951, while reporting that the quality of sightings was improving. As time went on, the public began to pay less attention to sightings. The Air Force ended one investigation program (Project Sign) and began another program with different priorities.[21]

As the new "Project Grudge" began in 1949, the program's public title was Project Saucer. Project Grudge began to implement the new emphasis that reflected General Vandenberg's no extraterrestrial hypothesis. Despite Air Force insistence that there was nothing to be concerned about, commercial pilots, military personnel, and a small number of scientists were publicly acknowledging aerial phenomena that they could not explain.[22] The public was seeing fewer unexplained objects in the sky, but more sightings were occurring near sensitive military, nuclear installations, and other civilian and military restricted airspace.

At the time, many sensitive military facilities were in the State of New Mexico. New Mexico experienced numerous sightings around White Sands military area and other sensitive bases. Near the end of 1948, a phenomenon called "green fireballs" occurred almost exclusively over New Mexico airspace.

Despite a segment of the Air Force that wanted to continue to consider an extraterrestrial hypothesis, the Air Force came to the public conclusion that there was no basis for an extraterrestrial cause behind any sightings. From 1948 to 1951, the reported sightings dropped, and the public generally found comfort in the conclusions of Project Sign and Project Grudge. Publicly declared Air Force policy was that people who witness these extraordinary events were mistaken, delusional, or lying. No other explanation could justify the phenomenon. Reports that were designated "unknown" would have prosaic explanations only if the investigators had more information.

---

21   Ruppelt, Edward, J., The Report on Unidentified Flying Objects (Original 1956 Edition) Doubleday & Company, reissued Cosimo Classics (2011).

22   National Investigations Committee on Aerial Phenomenon (NICAP), Richard H. Hall (Editor), The UFO Evidence (1964), reprint Barnes & Noble Books (1997), pp. 49–55. This book was originally prepared for Congress by NICAP to provide sighting information and evidence to encourage Congress to hold hearings into the UFO/UAP phenomenon.

Eventually, the phenomenon reasserted itself. In 1952, the number of sightings increased dramatically. The summer of 1952 saw some of the most disturbing sightings to date. According to one source, the 158 leading newspapers in the country published approximately 16,000 items about flying saucers during a six-month period in 1952.[23] Even restricted airspace above Washington D.C. became a target of the phenomenon.[24] For a two-week period, Washington D.C. had many visual sightings that were confirmed on radar. At least one radar-confirmed sighting was over the White House.

The Truman Administration asked the CIA to review the subject. Between August and December of 1952, the CIA discussed options to deal with the phenomenon by consulting with the Air Force. The CIA and Air Force eventually developed a joint approach to the flying saucer "problem." By the end of 1952, it settled on convening a panel of scientists to do a four-day study of the matter and report back to the Deputy Director of Central Intelligence. The idea of a long-term scientific study was rejected in favor of a study that called no actual witnesses but mostly listened to Air Force and CIA personnel discuss a preselected set of cases. During the transition between Presidents Truman and Eisenhower, the CIA-appointed panel was convened to study flying saucers from January 14–17, 1953.

Once formed, the panel's chair was Cal Tech physicist H.P. Robertson. Another member was UC Berkeley physicist Luis Alvarez. Both had studied the World War II "foo fighters." Despite the CIA website stating that the panel was made up of non-military scientists, each Robertson Panel member worked for the military before and after being on the secret panel. All panelists held security clearances,

---

23 Ruppelt, Edward, J., The Report on Unidentified Flying Objects (Original 1956 Edition) Doubleday & Company, reissued Cosimo Classics (2011). Before the Internet and 24-hour cable news, an important research tool, used by the Air Force, were newspaper clipping services. They would supply the subscriber with stories from national and local newspapers about any topic. They did not cover every newspaper, but a substantial portion of the nation's newspapers. This helped the Air Force keep up with sighting reports.

24 Clark, Jerome, The UFO Book: Encyclopedia of the Extraterrestrial (1998), Visible Ink Press, pp. 653–662.

working on highly-classified programs. They were early members of the military-industrial complex.

After completion of the panel's work, its report was distributed to various military and executive agencies. Some were given more information than others. The recommendations to "debunk" persons who filed reports and to "watch" private UFO organizations were only given to the Defense Department. While distributed within the government, the CIA panel report was kept secret until 1956 when retired Captain Edward Ruppelt disclosed its existence.[25] Various versions of the report have been disclosed through public records (Freedom of Information Act (FOIA)) requests. The panel report's[26] distribution and impacts on government policy has never been fully made public. However, it is clear from declassified records and numerous related incidents that the policies of the federal government still mirror the Robertson Panel's recommendations.

This report, in the eyes of many, led to a new "dark ages" of UFO investigations where the Air Force abandoned even the pretense of scientific effort. While the Air Force continued to retain astronomer, Dr. J. Alan Hynek, explanations of serious cases became farcical. Dr. James E. McDonald, professor of astrophysics (University of Arizona), commented upon this shift as follows:

"As nearly as I can tell, the January 1953, Robertson Panel Report marked the turning point with its regrettable decision to leave the UFO problem in the hands of a group not primarily concerned with scientific matters, and at the same time to have them shift to debunking policies to decrease public interest in the entire matter. It remains a very puzzling period, and an extremely important one in the history of UFO studies."[27]

---

25 Ruppelt, E., The Report on Unidentified Flying Objects, readaclassic.com (2010), reprint of 1956 original version, pp. 190, 211–215.

26 The Report is alternately known as the "Robertson Panel Report," after its Panel Chair Dr. Harold Percy Robertson or the "Durant Report," after the Panel's Secretary Frederick Durant.

27 National Investigations Committee on Aerial Phenomena (NICAP), United States Air Force (Projects Grudge and Bluebook Reports 1–12, Forward @ p. ix, Washington D.C. (1968)).

After the classified report was finished, portions were circulated within the government.[28] It helped assure high-level policy makers (military, intelligence community, Civil Defense, and State Department) that the phenomenon was not real. The panel report recommended that witnesses should be "debunked" and organizations who study the phenomenon should be placed under surveillance.[29] As discussed above, the more problematic recommendations with civil rights implications were only sent to a smaller sub-group.

As stated by University of Arizona professor, Dr. James E. McDonald,[30] the Robertson Panel Report marked a sea change in the way persons were treated who advocated the extraterrestrial hypothesis. The same treatment applied to eyewitnesses, even though most eyewitnesses had little interest in the phenomenon before their sighting. While the Air Force had issued reports with similar conclusions about the nature of the phenomenon, the Robertson Panel Report gave license to discriminatory treatment of groups and individuals who had witnessed or advocated the reality of the phenomenon. By the end of 1953, the Air Force issued a companion policy that required commercial airline pilots to report every UFO to the Air Force. The policy required witnesses who filed the report to avoid talking to the press since discussion of the sighting would be considered a leak of a classified government report. After the Air Force and CIA policies were circulated, reports from witnesses with trained observational skills began to dry up. The public reports made by trained professionals became "professional suicide" for those brave enough to still step forward. Any public witnesses that reported what they saw to military or civilian authorities had their views misrepresented and, if they presented compelling physical evidence, it would be kept by

---

28 Ruppelt, E., The Report on Unidentified Flying Objects, readaclassic.com (2010), reprint of 1956 original version @ fn. 26.

29 Report of Scientific Advisory Panel on Unidentified Flying Objects Convened by the Office of Scientific Intelligence, CIA. January 14–18, 1953, Tab "A", January 17, 1953; http://www.cufon.org/cufon/robert.htm ("Robertson Panel" or "Durant Report").

30 Dr. McDonald was one of the early climate scientists that studied the effects of pollution on the ozone layer. He wrote some of the most prescient scientific papers on the subject.

the Air Force or returned with the most interesting photos or film segments removed.

In 1954, the Air Force conducted a briefing with the major commercial air carriers in Los Angeles. At the briefing, the UFO reporting process was explained. The airline representatives were cautioned not to allow their pilots to publicly discuss their UFO sightings.[31]

Their rationale was that the Soviet Union could use flying saucer "hysteria" to mask an attack on the United States. The Robertson Panel was made up of high-quality physical scientists who worked on weapons development, but none had a background in psychology. They had no expert testimony about the psychological impacts of UFO/UAP sightings. One of the main findings of the panel was as follows:

> "That the continued emphasis on the reporting of these phenomena does, in these parlous times, result in a threat to the orderly functioning of the protective organs of the body politic."[32]

While the CIA study started as a referral from the Truman White House to determine what was behind these airspace incursions, the ultimate result was a policy to limit public discussion of these mysterious objects because of the threat caused by those who made the reports. A CIA Office of Scientific Intelligence 1953 yearend report on the effectiveness of the Robertson Panel policy recommendations lamented the fact that two books, *Flying Saucers From Outer Space* (Kehoe) and

---

31 National Investigations Committee on Aerial Phenomenon (NICAP), Richard H. Hall (Editor), The UFO Evidence (1964), reprint Barnes & Noble Books (1997), p. 134.

32 Report of Scientific Advisory Panel on Unidentified Flying Objects Convened by Office of Scientific Intelligence CIA January 14–18, 1953, Tab "A" (NICAP Declassified Version). https://jplufo.com/durant-report-robertson-panel-cufon-version/ (https://archive.org/search.php?query=CIA-RDP81R00560R000100030027-0). As this book was going to print, the CIA unveiled a new website. As a result, many relevant documents were no longer accessible. Citations to CIA documents will be made in two forms. The first citation will be to a website (jplufo.com) with a copy of the government document. The second citation will be to the CIA original citation in case the link to the document is restored.

The Flying Saucers Have Landed (Leslie & Adamski), were published in 1953 about the phenomenon.[33]

The Robertson Panel set internal government policy to discourage people from reporting UFO/UAPs. Persons who came forward to report a sighting were to be "debunked" for fear of causing "mass hysteria." Private organizations that were being formed to study flying saucers were supposed to be "watched" with unfounded concerns about their "loyalty" to the United States.[34]

The panel concluded that no sighting was of an actual unidentified foreign object. Each report was made by someone who was mistaken, lying, or delusional. Given enough evidence, all sightings could be explained using scientific knowledge that existed in 1953. Whether the panel came to the appropriate scientific conclusion or not, its method of investigation was flawed and some of its recommendations had serious civil liberty implications.

The panel never interviewed a single eyewitness. It never sought additional information about cases specified as "unknown" after an Air Force investigation. The Robertson Panel never talked to trained observers such as commercial airline pilots or military personnel who actually witnessed the phenomenon firsthand. As discussed earlier, there were highly credible reports from commercial airline pilots. The Robertson Panel concentrated on 15 cases, only nine of which are specifically referred to in the declassified version of the report.

The panel's analysis never deviated from pre-selected cases presented by CIA and Air Force staff. The threat did not come from outer space aliens or a foreign adversary, it came from American citizens who have either seen, studied, or believe in flying saucers. They constitute "a threat to the orderly functioning of the protective organs of the body politic." The government itself was threatened by these beliefs. The

---

33 https://jplufo.com/doc_0005515979-2/ (https://www.cia.gov/library/readingroom/docs/DOC_0005515979.pdf).

34 Report of Scientific Advisory Panel on Unidentified Flying Objects Convened by the Office of Scientific Intelligence, CIA. January 14–18, 1953, Part VI (Concerns and Suggestions of the Panel), pp. 23–24 (Unofficial Investigating Groups). https://jplufo.com/durant-report-robertson-panel-cufon-version/

government response was aimed at its own people. Actual investigation took a back seat to these questionable methods of inquiry.

NICAP's Congressional Hearing Requests are Rebuffed (1956–1964)

The UFO/UAP phenomenon continued to be part of the American experience in the late 1950s and early 1960s. Sightings still occurred but there were fewer trained observers that talked to the press. However, two camps developed that each defined the way that most Americans perceived the phenomenon.

On one side was the contactee movement and on the other were national organizations that grew out of the post-1947 flying saucer clubs. Each side had its dedicated supporters. The public at-large tended to lump the two factions together. In fact, there was crossover between these two groups. One looked for respectability, while the other made claims that were hard to document and even harder to believe. Rather than relying on newspapers, radio, or television to attract adherents, book sales and organization newsletters sent to dues-paying members were their main method of support.

In the early 1950s, the contactee movement got off the ground with George Adamski's story of alleged alien contact.[35] Mr. Adamski was the first of several contactees who claimed to have met with visitors from Venus and other planets in the solar system. Adamski's Venusians were beautiful human-looking creatures who came to Earth to warn about our use of nuclear weapons and preached a message of peace. Adamski held large lectures and had a loyal following of adherents. He was soon followed by many other contactees who lectured and sold books about their adventures. Little evidence supported their claims, but their claims to be the chosen humanity's emissaries attracted much attention.

---

35   Leslie, Desmond; Adamski, George, Flying Saucers Have Landed, (1953) (New York: British Book Centre).

The CIA, after the Robertson Panel, lamented the publication of books about flying saucers while it was working with the Air Force to lower the profile of UFO/UAPs. An Agency-declassified 1953 year-end report about the impact of the Robertson Panel policies decried publication of two UFO/UAP books.[36] Discussing the Adamski story, the CIA memo found a potentially positive impact of his book: "Fortunately, the later book (Leslie & Adamski's) is so nonsensical and obviously fraudulent that it may actually calm down public reaction."[37]

The other book that concerned the CIA and Air Force was written by retired Marine Major Donald Keyhoe. Keyhoe was to become a central player in the other movement that started in the late 1940s and early 1950s. Groups called "flying saucer clubs" began sprouting up around the United States. Two of these early groups, Civilian Saucer Investigators-Los Angeles (CSI-LA) and the Aerial Phenomenon Research Organization (APRO) were mentioned by the Robertson Panel as organizations that needed to be "watched."[38] These two groups needed to be "watched because of their potentially great influence on mass thinking if mass sightings should occur."[39] The Robertson Panel, while debunking UFO/UAPs, was concerned about future mass sightings.

CSI-LA was a small organization run from the kitchen tables of its members. Mailed newsletters were how these groups kept their members informed of the latest developments. CSI-LA stood out because of its roster of scientists and engineers that reviewed cases. Most worked in the budding aerospace industry. This expertise made them a valuable source of information for publications like *Life* and *Time* magazines. These magazines gave this small group of volunteers an international reputation. The publications were on the coffee tables of America

---

36 https://jplufo.com/doc_0005515979-2/ (https://www.cia.gov/library/readingroom/docs/DOC_0005515979.pdf)

37 Id. @ Section 5.

38 Report of Scientific Advisory Panel on Unidentified Flying Objects Convened by the Office of Scientific Intelligence, CIA. January 14–18, 1953, Part II (Comments and Suggestions of the Panel), pp. 23–24 (Unofficial Investigating Groups). https://jplufo.com/durant-report-robertson-panel-cufon-version/

39 Id.

households and were a primary source for news. CSI-LA was the first group that drew CIA scrutiny immediately after the Robertson Panel issued its recommendations.[40] CIA scrutiny of CSI-LA members in the defense industry led to an exodus of its best technically gifted members. The organization ceased operations by the Spring of 1954.

APRO was the other organization singled out to be watched. It linked up small flying saucer clubs around the country and became the first nationwide UFO/UAP organization. Its focus was on UFO/UAP sightings and it shied away from the sensational claims of the contactees. Its founders were Coral and Jim Lorenzen. Coral worked as a civilian employee for the military which could possibly explain the organization's reluctance to engage in a call for congressional hearings.

In October 1956, another national organization was founded with a board of directors that included some very prominent figures. The National Investigations Committee on Aerial Phenomena (NICAP) pressed for congressional hearings about UFO/UAPs. Donald Keyhoe, former CIA Director Vice Admiral Roscoe Hillenkoetter, and former Army Gen. Albert Coady Wedemeyer were board members.

The call for congressional hearings and the near instant credibility that the NICAP gained from its prominent players created a problem for the Air Force. Keyhoe's 1950 book, *Flying Saucers Are Real*, sold over half a million copies. His 1953 book, *Flying Saucers From Outer Space*, was one of the books that concerned the CIA in the yearend 1953 report on the success of the Robertson Panel policies. Keyhoe used Air Force files to document his book and convince many Americans that the government was hiding the truth.

NICAP lobbied Congress to hold hearings and many elected representatives were willing to grant that request. The Air Force spent much of the late 1950s and 1960s trying to keep hearings from happening. UFO/UAPs were a public relations nightmare for the Air Force and it spent much effort trying to get other agencies to take the "UFO

---

40   https://jplufo.com/2-9-1953-la-office-visit-dr-riedel-cia-rdp81r00560r000100030023-4/
      (https://www.cia.gov/library/readingroom/docs/CIA-RDP81R00560R000100030023-4.pdf).

problem" off their hands. In January 1958, NICAP was able to persuade Senator John McClellan (D-Ark.) into inquiring about hearings on UFO/UAPs in front of the Government Operations Subcommittee he chaired. The Air Force pushed back, claimed there was no reason to hold hearings.[41] The fact that hearings were held would create "uncontrolled publicity."[42] No hearings were held.

This did not end the Air Force concern. In June 1958, Representative John E. Henderson (R-Ohio) had read a Captain (ret.) Edward Ruppelt book about flying saucers and sent written questions to the Air Force about the phenomenon. In response, the Air Force briefed Henderson and several other congressmen about the subject. Parts of the classified Robertson Panel Report were distributed as part of the briefing.

The requests continued that summer. In addition to a three-term representative (Henderson), Congressman John McCormick (D-Mass.) requested UFO/UAP hearings later in the Summer of 1958. McCormick was no "back-bencher." In 1940, he received the backing of Congressman Sam Rayburn (D-Tex.) and was elected House Majority Leader, second in line behind Speaker Rayburn. McCormick became Speaker in 1962 upon Rayburn's death and held that post until his retirement in 1971. While his request was made by the House Subcommittee on Atmospheric Phenomena, it was his House leadership position that commanded attention. McCormick wanted a week-long closed hearing with "unrecorded, names of witnesses to be held in confidence."[43] He asked that Donald Menzel, Donald Keyhoe, and Edward Ruppelt be called as witnesses. The Air Force was not concerned about the testimony of Donald Menzel who was a UFO skeptic, Harvard professor, and contract employee of the National Security Agency. Also, there was little concern about former Air Force Captain Edward Ruppelt. However, the Air Force was concerned about Donald Keyhoe, NICAP official and bestselling author about UFO/UAPs.

---

41   Jacobs, David, UFO Controversy in America (1975), Signet Books, p. 141.
42   Id.
43   Id. @ p. 142.

McCormick began by stating that the proceedings were not really a hearing, but a request for information.[44] After an opening set of presentations by the Air Force, it was decided that no more witnesses need be called. This prevented Donald Keyhoe from presenting information to the subcommittee. The Air Force presented information, but no other source was heard in the closed proceeding. McCormick's subcommittee finished its inquiry and took the word of the Air Force.

In the summer of 1960, other attempts were made to secure congressional briefings. Several members of the House and Senate pushed for hearings and the Air Force went into another flurry of activity to try to stop the effort. After briefing members of Congress, some in groups, over the next several years, no formal hearings were called. While not all members who were briefed had confidence in the Air Force's handling of the phenomenon, none were able to muster enough support for open hearings. All the while, the Air Force sent a member of its public relations unit around the country for media appearances to downplay the UFO/UAP phenomenon.[45] By 1960, one member of Congress that was not convinced by the Air Force was House Majority Leader John McCormick. However, until the next triggering event was to surface, no hearings, closed or open, were held.

A New UFO/UAP Wave Gives Life to Hearing Requests and a "Scientific" Study (1965–1969)

In 1965, the number of monthly UFO/UAP sighting reports to Project Blue Book increased dramatically. The increase gave new life to NICAP's requests for congressional hearings. An increase in sightings was one of the worries of the 1953 CIA Robertson Panel. On this issue, they recommended as follows:

"The Panel took cognizance of the existence of such groups

---

44 Id @ p. 142.
45 Id. @ pp. 154–159.

as the 'Civilian Flying Saucer Investigators' (Los Angeles) and the "Aerial Phenomena Research Organization" (Wisconsin). It was believed that such organizations should be watched because of their potentially great influence on mass thinking if widespread sightings should occur. The apparent irresponsibility and the possible use of such groups for subversive purposes should be kept in mind."[46] (emphasis added.)

With the 1965 case increase, the fears of the Air Force were realized. Since NICAP was formed in 1956, it was not mentioned by the Robertson Panel as an organization to "watch." However, it was a greater challenge to the Air Force in 1965. Dr. David Jacobs, a Temple University Historian, explained the change in landscape in 1965, as follows:

"The impetus for this turning point was the one unknown variable, and the crux of all the controversy-UFO sightings. Although ATIC recorded sighting reports at an average rate of 30 to 50 per month for the first six months of 1965, it received 135 reports for July and 262 in August. This began a wave that continued until the middle of 1967. The increase in reports prompted widespread press and public criticism of the Air Force UFO program and an outpouring of popular articles and books on UFOs."[47]

The CIA and Air Force concern of a new wave came true. Much of the press had begun to ask the same questions that had been asked during the 1952 wave. The 1952 wave led to the formation of the CIA Robertson Panel. This 1965–67 wave would have similar results.

Members of Congress started calling for hearings and a scientific

---

46 Report of Scientific Advisory Panel on Unidentified Flying Objects Convened by the Office of Scientific Intelligence, CIA. January 14–18, 1953, PART II: (Concerns and Suggestions of the Panel), pp. 23–24 (Unofficial Investigating Groups). https://jplufo.com/durant-report-robertson-panel-cufon-version/
47 Jacobs, David, UFO Controversy in America, Signet Books (1975), p. 171.

review of the phenomenon. One event, not much different than many other sightings, changed the trajectory of the struggle. It happened in Michigan in 1966. A mass UFO/UAP sighting at Hillsdale College brought into the spotlight the lengths to which the Air Force would go to come up with explanations to fit within the Air Force's three categories of cases: mistaken identity, delusion, or fabrication.

On March 20, 1966, at least 87 Hillsdale College students watched a four-hour display by a UFO/UAP that flew in and around the campus. Others also saw the same football-shaped object at close distance on that night. On the next day, a similar craft was witnessed by two police officers and a farmer near the college.

Project Blue Book dispatched Dr. J. Allen Hynek, its science advisor, to the scene. Prior to his arrival, the nation's media had descended on the area and, when Hynek arrived, he had trouble investigating with so many reporters present. When pressed for an explanation, Dr. Hynek speculated that decomposed vegetation may have been the cause. The press seized on the term "swamp gas" and ran with it. Media condemnation of the flippant explanation was swift. *Life Magazine* put an eight-page story about the sightings and the Air Force response on living room coffee tables throughout the U.S.

Two local congressmen, Weston E. Vivian (D-Mich.) and Gerald R. Ford (R-Mich.) called for immediate congressional hearings. House Minority Leader Ford, who had just served on the Warren Commission two years before, was an influential voice in Congress. At the time, Ford stated that: "the American public deserved a better explanation than that thus far given by the Air Force....to establish credibility" about UFOs.[48]

Acting quickly, the House Armed Services Committee began an open hearing about the subject on April 5, 1966. Three Air Force representatives were the only witnesses. Stating that he had not cleared his testimony with the Air Force, Dr. Hynek testified that the UFO

---

48   Id. @ p. 181.

phenomenon needed scientific review and called for a scientific study of the subject by civilian scientists. During questioning, when Air Force Secretary Harold Brown stated he was considering whether to conduct a scientific study, the Armed Services Committee ran with the idea and requested that it be implemented by the Air Force.

After the Hillsdale sightings and the lengthy story in *Life Magazine* the week before, the Air Force was given a new assignment. One that could put an end to the debate, one way or the other. The Air Force began a search for an academic institution to sponsor the study. After many schools turned the Air Force down, an agreement was reached with the University of Colorado for a $500,000 study. It was announced by the Air Force on October 7, 1966. Physicist Edward U. Condon would head the project that was popularly known as the "Condon Committee." Assistant Dean of the Graduate School Robert Low would be the project coordinator.

NICAP and the UFO community generally hailed the announcement. So did Project Blue Book scientific consultant J. Allen Hynek. Most hoped that the study would confirm their particular beliefs, skeptics and believers alike. However, the study would get off to a rocky start.

At first, there was little coordination of how to do an investigation. One staff member resigned early over an emphasis that focused on the psychology of the witness and not their sighting. Robert Low, the project coordinator, was caught assuring another University of Colorado professor in correspondence that the study would not advocate an extraterrestrial hypothesis as part of the final outcome. While Low would later attempt to bring balance to the study and consider past cases in the Air Force files, Dr. Edward Condon made several public statements that denigrated serious consideration of the ET visitation possibility. At the same time, he spent most of his efforts looking at contactee cases and obvious hoaxes. Overall, he hardly participated but wrote the conclusion section. The conclusions matched the direction he was given by Air Force Col. Robert Hippler who oversaw the Air Force grant for the study. In correspondence to project coordinator Robert Low, Hippler stated that the Air Force wanted the study to help them get out of the UFO business.[49]

Edward Condon began to take a greater role as the study's deadline grew near. He terminated two team members who made Low's letter public which prejudged the "no E.T." outcome. While speaking to members of the American Chemical Society, Condon stated that the purpose of the study was to get the Air Force out of the UFO/UAP business.[50] Condon, throughout the study, made public statements about the lack of value in studying UFOs. These statements hurt team morale and raised questions about the impartial nature of the study. Two national articles were published during the study about its problems.[51]

During the study, the House Committee on Science and Astronautics held a "symposium" on the UFO question. The committee heard from six witnesses[52] and received papers from others about the debate. The July 29, 1968 hearing discussed the issues from several perspectives in what could be called a general inquiry about the subject. At the end of the hearing/symposium, the witnesses were invited to discuss things they felt were relevant. Astronomer Carl Sagan began by explaining that the Air Force radar tracking of possible space objects would discount those that did not proceed in a straight line, the profile of a missile launch. Objects under 90,000 feet were also ignored. Data that did not fit this narrow profile would be discarded. However, this was the type of data that would help understand the phenomena. If the Air Force kept this data, it would help with our understanding of unknown aerial phenomena. The panelists who were arguing for further study agreed with skeptic/agnostic Dr. Sagan. Software adjustments could make more data available.

---

49 Swords, Michael, D.; Powell, Robert, UFOs and Government: A Historical Inquiry, Anomalist Books (2012), p. 331
50 Id. @ p. 201.
51 Boffey, Philip, "UFO Project: Trouble on the Ground," Science Magazine, July 26, 1968: pp. 339–342; Fuller, John, "Flying Saucer Fiasco," Look Magazine, May 14, 1968: pp. 58–63.
52 Jacobs, David, UFO Controversy in America, Signet Books (1975), pp. 160-170.

However, there was no follow-up to this recommendation. Shortly after the hearing, Congress took its summer recess. Other matters took priority. 1968 was a year filled with many issues: a presidential election, civil unrest, and the height of the Viet Nam War. The UFO subject got lost among these more pressing issues.

A week before the 1968 election, the Condon Committee delivered their report to the Air Force. It was later distributed to the public in January 1969. As with the Robertson Panel Report in 1953, the final report was distributed to a new administration from a different political party than the one that ordered it. The "conclusions and recommendations" were written by Edward Condon who actually did little or no work on the substantive portions of the report. The conclusion mirrored his personal opinions that he had been telegraphing for more than a year before its issuance. Despite the stamp of approval from the science editor for the *New York Times* in the forward, much of the report contradicted the conclusions drawn by Condon. For example, the conclusions of one prominent case stated:

> "In conclusion, although conventional or natural explanations certainly cannot be ruled out, the probability of such seems low in this case and the probability that at least one genuine UFO was involved appears to be fairly high."[53]

This 1956 case conclusion is one example of a contradiction between the report's conclusion and the statement of nothing of scientific interest can be found from further study of UFOs. The statistical breakdowns in the report point out similar contradictions between the body of the report and the conclusion.

However, the stamp of approval from Walter Sullivan of the *New York Times* and the National Academy of Sciences, who vouched for the scientific methods used, gave the Air Force what it wanted. On January

---

53   i.e. The Black Vault website: https://documents2.theblackvault.com/documents/ntis/CondonReport-Complete.pdf, p. 246.

19, 1970, the Air Force officially terminated Project Blue Book. The Air Force no longer accepted UFO sighting reports. Despite the fact that *Science Magazine* ran an article on the chaos in the management of the study, these endorsements were the final word and very few people looked behind the curtain.

This conclusion ended any serious scientific inquiries for the foreseeable future. No researcher could seriously propose a study and expect to be funded. While sightings of UFO/UAP phenomena continue to this day, the willingness of scientists of the stature of an atmospheric physicist like Dr. James McDonald would no longer pursue study of this phenomenon for the foreseeable future.

Historic Patterns for Dealing with UFO/UAP Public Policy

Congress routinely relies upon federal agencies to keep them informed on emerging issues. Historically, federal agencies have a relationship of trust with the congressional committees that have oversight of their budget and operations. While partisan issues and controversies can lead to distrust between federal agencies and Congress, the UFO/UAP issue does not fit the normal partisan wrangling profile. First, it has traditionally come up as an issue of defense significance. When there is a genuine defense need that emerges, partisanship usually takes a backseat. This is not the type of issue, such as a costly weapons system; polarizing social issue; or a potential armed conflict that does not have bipartisan support. This is an issue that does not divide us on partisan lines. Interest in the subject is not restricted to one party or interest group. Historically, the congressional inquiries into the subject have been fairly equal across party lines. The most recent interest has come from former Senate Majority Leader Harry Reid (D-Nev.) and Acting Senate Select Intelligence Committee Chair Marco Rubio (R-Fla.).

Yet, the historic public record shows a reticence by the Air Force and the CIA to provide basic information to Congress until they have no choice. Requests for information about the UFO/UAP phenomenon have followed several disturbing patterns. It is critical that the 117th Congress understand these patterns and how they may affect Congress' ability to address the issue with the best interests of the American people in mind.

THE SLOW WALK

UFO/UAP inquiries have routinely met with delayed responses from the defense and intelligence communities. After the 1952 wave that included dramatic sightings over Washington D.C., President Truman made a referral in late July. The CIA met with the Air Force on a regular basis and delayed coming up with a formal response until December 1952. Yet, in August 1952, the Air Force and CIA had decided that the referral would study the psychological warfare implications of UFO/UAP sightings rather than looking at the underlying cause of the phenomenon, as Truman had requested.[54] Because of the delay in forming the scientific panel, it was too late for Truman to make any policy changes to match his original inquiry. The slow walk of the request meant that the Truman Administration did not have the benefit of the results. The new administration did not share it with Congress. The urgency felt in July 1952 was eclipsed by other matters and the new Congress did not address the issue.

The same pattern emerged in the late 1960s with the Condon Report. The report, received on October 31, 1968, was not circulated until January 1969. This was after another change in administrations. At least in 1969, the Air Force did not hide it with a classified designation. However, the delay between issuance and its public release separates the issuance of the report and the spike in sightings that led a congressional committee to ask for the study.

Today, we do not know whether the DNI and SecDef will follow the

---

54 https://jplufo.com/doc_0000015343-august-4-1952-control-of-ufo-question-2/ (https://www.cia.gov/library/readingroom/docs/DOC_0000015343.pdf).

historic pattern of delay. The report is due on June 25, 2021. This date came about through a very tortured history. The Senate's version of the Intelligence Authorization Bill (S. 3905) was eventually subsumed into the House of Representatives' version. The combined version was adopted as part of the combined COVID relief package and the funding of federal government for fiscal year 2021. (Consolidated Appropriations Act of 2021, Division W—Intelligence Authorization Act for Fiscal Year 2021.) By its terms under Section 3 of Division W, the consolidated bill incorporates the report of Senator Marco Rubio (R-Fla.) which contained the direction for the UAP Report. In addition, after the Senate Select Intelligence Committee voted on its UFO/UAP report request, the Defense Department authorized Deputy Defense Secretary David L. Norquist to oversee the UAP Task Force. Norquist's normal responsibilities are budgetary and fiscal matters. An interesting choice to supervise a UFO/UAP report. However, Norquist left office within a week of the change in presidential administrations. How the new administration will handle this request for a report is unknown.

Even if the report is prepared in a timely manner, it is likely that the report will not answer the questions of the referral. The committee comments asked that the Director of National Intelligence (DNI) coordinate with the military branches and the 18 intelligence agencies. The extent of the new DNI's efforts are yet unknown. It is still an open question as to whether the new administration will follow old patterns or set a new course that includes Congress as a full partner.

METHODS TO DELAY CONGRESSIONAL INQUIRIES

Most interactions between Congress and agencies or service branches are staff-to-staff. Congressional inquiries on behalf of constituents or as part of committee duties are conducted by congressional staffers who obtain information to help the member of Congress on the issues of importance. Congressional offices come to rely on the information they receive in this manner. A level of trust hopefully develops. For members of the Armed Services and Select Intelligence Committees, these interactions guide the questions that a member asks at hearings and helps form the basis for determining support or opposition for issues before each committee. Partisanship can often color these exchanges of information when the member is from a different party than the executive branch.

When it comes to the UFO/UAP issue, the responses to Congress mostly have the feel of a hyper-partisan issue regardless of the party in power. Both Republicans and Democrats have found themselves on the wrong end of these exchanges. The past interactions between members of Congress and the Defense Department or intelligence community discussed above are not the only examples of this behavior.

There are many instances of members of Congress being told to leave the subject alone. An example of this is Senator Barry Goldwater (R-Az.) who was prevented from learning what the Air Force knew about the question. He asked Air Force General Curtis LeMay about UFO/UAPs. LeMay warned him off the entire subject, telling a sitting senator never to ask about the subject again.[55]

Another example is a sighting by Senator Richard Russell (D-Ga.). In 1955, he was part of an American delegation on a train traveling through the Soviet Union on the way to Prague, Czechoslovakia. According to staffers traveling with him, they saw two saucer-shaped objects pass over the countryside. Immediately thereafter, one of the Soviet officials rushed into the American delegation's coach car and shut the curtains. Later, a reporter asked Senator Russell to comment on the incident and he responded:

"I have discussed this matter with the affected agencies, and they are of the opinion that it is not wise to publicize this matter at this time."[56]

---

55 https://www.youtube.com/watch?v=gPFBg1NNUBU
56 https://www.express.co.uk/news/weird/578055/
    Senior-US-senator-s-report-TWO-UFOs-covered-up-secret-documents

The question becomes: when is the "time" to discuss this phenomenon? It has been 65 years since Senator Russell made this statement. The UFO/UAP phenomenon has not gone away, yet the policy remains the same. The public government policy is that all UFO/UAP reports are made by people who are mistaken, fabricating, or delusional. UFO/UAPs have nothing to add to our scientific knowledge and are unworthy of serious study. Yet, the same subject is classified at the highest levels and FOIA requests for information about 75-year-old events are still heavily redacted. It is a striking contradiction. The phenomenon is not real, but congressional access to information about it is highly-classified. Congressional inquiries have been rejected directly or through other means since World War II.

The history of congressional requests for UFO/UAP information shows how delays and outright refusals are standard practice for the Defense Department and intelligence agencies. When there is a member inquiry about the subject, the first instinct of the Executive Branch is to either ignore or take time responding. After delays do not make the inquiry go away, the first option is to hold an individual briefing with the requesting member. Even though most occur off-the-record, the member is only given public information and no information beyond that, regardless of the member's authority to access classified information.

If there is a push for a hearing, an informal briefing is given without access to any records, policies, or information that raises any doubt about the official policy. If more than one member requests information, informal briefings as a group are held with no additional information than is already in the public domain. Most requests for information are rebuffed, even if the subject matter is relevant to the member's committee assignment, *i.e.* Armed Services and UFO/UAP military base intrusions.

When questions were raised by enough members, the subject would be discussed by Air Force and intelligence personnel in a committee setting. Usually, it was the chair of the committee that would approach the subject timidly and defer to the Air Force representatives. These types of briefings are usually informal and don't use the typical hearing process. The 1968 House Armed Services hearing was described by the chair as a "symposium." It resulted in a debate between skeptics and advocates of serious study. The most prominent skeptic at the hearing was Professor Donald Menzel of Harvard. The independence of Menzel is questionable since, at the time, he was working for the National Security Agency. Menzel never mentioned his employment by the NSA to the Armed Services Committee holding the "seminar."

Congress has never held a public hearing in which actual witnesses presented information about their sightings. Congress has never heard from trained military witnesses about their sightings. These individuals could provide real time information about how service personnel respond to the potential threat. Whether in a classified setting or in public, Congress has yet to actually hear from the personnel who have had to react to these rare situations. This information is important because of the current policy to restrict information. This prevents service personnel from being prepared for a future incident. Without this firsthand knowledge, recommendations for programs, training, and procedures will be determined by the DNI and SecDef without any understanding of how the actual personnel who dealt with these issues reacted.

Overall, Congress has not used one of its only tools to find out how its expenditures will affect the performance of military personnel who encounter UFO/UAPs. Throughout the history of the phenomenon, our service personnel have been told not to discuss their sightings. The same advisement given to Senator Richard Russell in 1955. It was like being told to ignore the lessons learned after a sneak attack on our troops. No intelligence could be passed on to other commands so that they could learn lessons from the experiences.

If UFO/UAPs are a threat to our armed forces, why is our long-standing policy to ignore them? If Congress is to address the potential threat, it needs to learn from those who have been through these unique experiences. A policy that deliberately ignores a threat means one of two things. First, the policy of deliberate ignorance will have disastrous consequences in the case of an actual attack. Second, there is no actual threat and the long-term policy of maintaining ignorance of frontline troops is being continued for a reason that is unknown to Congress.

V

FLIR.MP4, GIMBAL.WMV, GOFAST.WMV AND HISTORIC PARALLELS

THE NAVY'S UAP TASK Force would not be in existence if it weren't for incidents captured on video by its pilots in 2004 and 2015. The declassified footage captures three incidents: FLIR, Gimbal, and GOFAST.[57] Each of these objects appears similar to previous cases presented to Congress. In 1964, NICAP submitted a briefing book (*The UFO Evidence*) to Congress that discussed many of the cases of interest that the UFO organization had investigated.[58] The parallels between the compilation of reports mentioned in NICAP's guide to Congress and today's reports should not be ignored. The types of objects; their performance characteristics; and manner of behavior are remarkably similar to sightings by trained observers from the 1940s and onward.

---

57 https://www.navair.navy.mil/foia/documents
58 National Investigations Committee on Aerial Phenomenon (NICAP), Richard H. Hall (Editor), *The UFO Evidence* (1964), reprint Barnes & Noble Books (1997).

November 2004 Nimitz Carrier Group Incidents

Possibly the most important evidence of the Nimitz Carrier Group encounters was not eyewitness accounts from fighter pilots. On Wednesday, November 10, 2004 and several days prior to the first air-to-air encounter, radar returns from the AN/Spy One phased array system on the Aegis-class cruiser U.S.S. Princeton began showing 50 or so unknown blips at 28,000 feet near San Clemente Island off the Southern California coast. They were heading south in groups of five to 10 objects moving at around 100 knots per hour. Since they did not appear to be a threat, the radar personnel monitored them but were not unduly concerned. However, the personnel in the U.S.S. Princeton Combat Information Center (CIC) began running diagnostic tests on the radar systems to determine if the objects were created by a system malfunction. The tests confirmed that the systems were not causing the objects. After the diagnostic tests were completed, the objects appeared even sharper on the display screens. As they became concerned, the crew began recording the system data showing these objects. The groups of identical objects continued south into the area reserved for air combat training at an altitude that the training was to take place.

On Sunday, November 14th, the Nimitz begins launching its F/A-18 Super Hornet fighters from the Black Aces Squadron for the air exercise. Worried about the latest group of unknown objects heading south from the Catalina Island area, the U.S.S. Princeton's CIC directs the first two planes off the Nimitz flight deck towards the nearest object. Considering that the group of objects was heading towards the area where the training was to take place, there was an air safety concern. The wing commander for the squadron and his wingman were vectored to the closest object's radar position. Upon arriving at this position, the two F/A 18 Super Hornets could not initially see the object. The wing commander looked down and saw the object hovering 50 feet above the water over a disturbance that indicated another unknown object was underwater.

At this point, the wing commander dove to near the surface while leaving the other fighter plane at 28,000 feet. It was later determined by the U.S.S. Princeton's radar that the unknown object had dropped from 28,000 feet to 50 feet in 0.78 seconds.[59] No known aircraft could have performed this maneuver without breaking apart and killing the pilot from the g-force. It also should have created multiple sonic booms. Once the wing commander arrived near the water's surface, the object did a "barrel roll" around his plane and returned to 28,000 feet. Thereafter, it continued on its original course to the south.

The wing commander's two-plane flight then flew to their combat air patrol points.[60] When the wing commander arrived at his CAP point, one of the objects was already there. A combat air patrol point is classified. The CAP point is the station that carrier fighter aircraft maintain to protect the carrier group. Yet, the object knew where CAP point was. As other aircraft from the Nimitz began arriving on station for the exercise, one of the unknown craft was caught on camera by another fighter jet. This became the FLIR.mp4 that shows part of the engagement with this plane. The Navy has a better quality and longer version of FLIR.mp4 which may have been shown to a few members of Congress. While recording the object, the pilot switched camera modes showing the object from the normal and infrared perspectives. The camera showed the same object in each mode used which lowers the possibility of a malfunction since each mode is generated by different equipment. It showed that there was no heat signature from the object that would indicate a power source. Radar data showed that they arrived on scene near San Clemente Island by dropping straight down from 80,000 feet and coming to a stop at 28,000 feet. This change in altitude mirrored the rapid altitude change in the first pilot

---

59   Public testimony also shows that a similar drop in altitude occurred that brought the objects down to 28,000 feet. The radar on the U.S.S. Princeton also witnessed a drop in altitude from 80,000 to 20,000 feet in 0.75 seconds.

60   A combat air patrol point (CAP point) is the location where the fighter planes are stationed to protect the carrier group. Each fighter jet goes to this location in the sky and slowly circles while they look for threats to the group.

engagement. After shadowing the fighters, the object captured on the FLIR.mp4 video left the area at a speed that none of the fighter pilots had ever witnessed. Experienced pilots have stated that they had never seen an object move so fast. As with other maneuvers, this rapid departure has many historical antecedents discussed in the 1964 NICAP book, *The UFO Evidence*.

The Nimitz objects were described as 40-foot-wide "tic tacs." This shape is consistent with other objects chronicled in the past. Ovoid or elliptical shape was a common description of unknown objects in the past. Not all UFO/UAPs are classic lenticular-shaped flying saucers.

ROOSEVELT 2014–2015 INCIDENTS

In 2014–2015, the U.S.S. Roosevelt was shadowed by many unknown objects. These objects were seen and captured on radar off the Atlantic Coast and similar craft shadowed the Roosevelt Carrier Group during combat operations in the Middle East. The Gimbal.wmv and GOFAST.wmv aircraft camera videos show a small portion of the sightings. One fighter pilot is heard exclaiming on the Gimbal.wmv video that there were a "fleet" of objects in the area. The objects shadowed the Roosevelt's F/A 18 Super Hornets on at least seven occasions. One pilot publicly stated that one unknown object passed between two Super Hornets in a two-plane flight. It approached the planes head-on and came within 110 feet as it made its high-speed pass. High-speed passes of aircraft have been witnessed by many commercial and military pilots over the years, including the 1948 Eastern Airlines flight on landing approach in Montgomery, Alabama. Hence, the air safety concerns. There are likely more aerial videos of these objects than Gimbal.wmv and GOFAST.wmv, along with other electronic surveillance information retained by the Navy, Air Force, or the intelligence community.

On April 26, 2013, the U.S. Coast Guard filmed an object at the Rafael Hernandez International Airport in Aguadilla, Puerto Rico similar to the object captured in the GOFAST.wmv.[61] This video was leaked to the public and has never been officially confirmed by the Coast Guard. Yet, it captures an object with similar flight characteristics as the GOFAST.wmv. No heat signature and no visible means of propulsion can be determined. This video is much clearer than the three Navy videos and shows the object performing maneuvers, above and below the surface of the North Atlantic Ocean. A Coast Guard helicopter tracks the object as it performs fast, erratic maneuvers over the airport, before heading to the nearby waters of the Atlantic off the north coast of Puerto Rico. It continued on a course in a westerly direction, diving in and out of the water without changing speed. While in the water, the object was joined by another identical object. The location of the Coast Guard object was relatively close to where the U.S.S. Roosevelt started having its encounters, about a year later.

Like the GOFAST.wmv, the 2013 Coast Guard footage looks like a small orb. No contrail or exhaust can be seen from any of the objects. None have propellers or a tail. While no Coast Guard personnel have come forward to claim to have witnessed the event, several Naval personnel have spoken publicly about their Roosevelt sightings.

HISTORICAL COMPARISON

The Nimitz, Roosevelt, and Coast Guard experiences are consistent with past sightings. In July 1964, Congress received its first briefing book on this subject. *The UFO Evidence*, by NICAP and edited by Richard H. Hall, was submitted to Congress to assist in NICAP's push for congressional hearings about UFO/UAPs.[62] This book details quality sighting reports, mostly from World War II through its 1964 publication. Within several months after its publication, the 1965–1967 wave of UFO/UAP sightings began in the United States.

---

61   https://www.youtube.com/watch?v=bxfdLkolCBQ
62   National Investigations Committee on Aerial Phenomenon (NICAP), Richard H. Hall (Editor), The UFO Evidence (1964), reprint Barnes & Noble Books (1997).

These increased incidents led to the first and only congressional hearing about UFO/UAPs in July 1968.

A comparison between the current sightings and past incidents can detect patterns that may guide the review of the anticipated report from the DNI. It can help establish whether the types of craft are consistent over the years. This comparison can help discover patterns of conduct that may shed light on the intent of the controllers of these unknown objects. While a comparison will not eliminate the possibility that the objects are of terrestrial origin, it will raise serious questions as to how another country developed these craft during the era of vacuum tubes and manual switches.

CRAFT TYPES

The UFO Evidence was written to present reports from credible witnesses and to try to detect patterns and common traits of the objects themselves. In the 1997 republication of the book, editor Richard H. Hall explained as follows:

> "In one sense, little has changed since 1964. Skeptics have hardened their attitudes, science and government seem unable to deal with the issue, and many people continue to make poor and unconvincing UFO reports. However, significant reports by highly-credible witnesses have multiplied. All of the patterns set forth in *The UFO Evidence* have been strongly confirmed by repeated observations, and several new patterns have emerged as well."[63]

As today, most reports and documentary evidence about UFO/UAPs were unconvincing. Yet, the increase in credible witness reports, considering the Navy witnesses that have come forward to discuss their

---

63   National Investigations Committee on Aerial Phenomenon (NICAP), Richard H. Hall (Editor), The UFO Evidence (1964), reprint Barnes & Noble Books (1997), foreword.

first person impressions of the objects, is as true today as it was in 1997 when Hall wrote the foreword to the reprint of *The UFO Evidence*. Navy fighter pilots and radar personnel are some of the best witnesses. They are trained to discriminate between aerial objects. Their training is intended to help them make critical decisions during stressful situations. So far, those witnesses that have come forward have consistent descriptions. This is true whether the descriptions of events were in the Pacific, Atlantic, or the Arabian Sea.

The earliest of the three videos was made in November 2004. It showed a 40-foot-wide tic tac-shaped object. In 1964, tic tacs were not a product. While they were introduced in 1968, the product's name was not changed to "Tic Tac" until 1970. Therefore, the term was not in common parlance at the time. A 1964 description of a tic tac-shaped object would probably use either "oval" or "elliptical."

According to the statistical analysis discussed in *The UFO Evidence*, from 1942 to 1963, 13% of UFO/UAP sightings were either oval or elliptical.[64] This was based on a sample size of 575 cases considered to be credible sightings. The largest category of the sample were disc-shaped (149) followed by light sources (140). Oval or elliptical sightings numbered 77 of 575. The fourth largest category in the survey sample.

The 2015 U.S.S. Roosevelt GOFAST.wmv was a spherical shape, as was the 2013 Coast Guard video. The 1942–1963 survey of 575 credible cases showed that spheres made up 96 cases or 17%. A portion of these cases were World War II "foo fighters" that were either self-luminating, bright spheres or metallic balls that flew off the wings of combat aircraft of both sides of the European and Pacific theatres. Most of these were drone-type objects and closely resemble the GOFAST and Coast Guard objects.

The Roosevelt Gimbal.wmv video displayed an object that was disc-like, but had a large protrusion from the center of the disc. The object displayed many of the same characteristics of the other types

---

64   Id. @ p. 143.

seen by the Navy and Coast Guard such as maneuverability without an apparent method of propulsion. *The UFO Evidence* has pictorial references of the shapes of different UFO/UAPs among its 575 cases presented. The Gimbal.wmv object most closely falls under the "flattened sphere" category. One of the variations under the "flattened sphere" sub-category shows a sharp, triangular peak on top of the sphere. The peak tapers to a point above the main structure of the craft. *The UFO Evidence,* under the representation, has an explanation that states: "sometimes with a peak." This representation closely resembles the Gimbal.wmv object, which had the same pointed peak.[65]

While the objects seen on the three declassified videos do not look like the classic flying saucer-type disc, they each resemble configurations that are listed in the July 1964 book, *The UFO Evidence.* Each type of object is one that was commonly sighted between 1942 and 1963. This demonstrates that each object seen in the three declassified videos has antecedents.

FLIGHT CHARACTERISTICS

The first encounter with a UFO/UAP by a pilot was the Nimitz's wing commander as training was about to begin. The first radar contacts showed the objects flying in formation. They flew in groups of five to 10 in the same formation each time. This behavior has historic parallels detailed in *The UFO Evidence.* It cites two witness accounts within two days of each other of UFO/UAPs "rendezvousing, then operating together."[66] The U.S.S. Princeton CIC recorded multiple, identical objects flying in formation, from north to south. They were always in formation when they would make abrupt altitude changes. Reforming at a different altitude and going forward in the same formation as before.

These sightings are also significant because of the erratic movements

---

65   Id. @ p. 144.
66   Id. @ pp. 13-15, 148.

of the objects. Many of these erratic maneuvers are part of a repeating pattern, such as circling around vehicles. The Nimitz wing commander experienced this firsthand. At the beginning of his encounter, he dove to near the ocean surface to reconnoiter the first visually sighted object. The object recognized his presence and engaged his F/A-18 Super Hornet. The 40-foot-long "tic tac" did a complete 360° pass around the aircraft. UFO/UAPs have used this maneuver in the past around a variety of objects.[67] Both ground-based vehicles and aircraft experienced having a UFO/UAP circle their vehicle.[68] Each case shows the maneuverability of these objects. It also can be inferred that the conduct was intended to demonstrate that the UFO/UAP object could not be mistaken for a traditional aircraft. Demonstrating the flight capabilities of a far superior craft has the effect of dampening any countermeasure that could escalate into a conflict. These high-speed flybys and aerobatic displays quickly demonstrate the gulf between these craft and our current level of technology.

The Coast Guard and GOFAST.wmv videos exhibit the same craft repeatedly witnessed during World War II off the wings of military aircraft on each side of the conflicts in the Pacific and European theaters of operation. Small balls of light at night and similar orbs during the day that exhibit intelligent control. They show an interest in our operations but take no aggressive actions. The threat comes mostly as a navigation hazard. Yet, the danger of these hazards mostly lies in our reactions to them.

For instance, the case of Captain Thomas Mantell is particularly instructive. Just after New Year's Day in 1948, an experienced combat pilot ignored the obvious safety risk to chase one of these objects beyond the range of his plane that was not equipped with oxygen. Captain Mantell was chasing after something that officially does not exist. Since it did not exist, pilots were given no training to prepare

---

67 Id. @ pp. 13-15, 148.
68 Id, @ pp. 10 (See: 5/29/50, 1/16/51, 1/20/51, 8/28/52 (case dates)), 12 (See: 10/3/58, 5/61), 20 (See: 3/29/52).

themselves for this eventuality. While training does not guarantee that a pilot will make the right call each time, it does help a pilot deal with this new situation with more confidence. When faced with a high-speed flyby of a UFO/UAP in restricted airspace, pilots on approach to land or flying in formation will be less likely to take evasive actions that could endanger themselves or those around them. Using past experiences, coupled with the more current examples, could help future pilots react appropriately when faced with a similar encounter.

Only using recent examples of UFO/UAP behavior limits the knowledge base of our government to deal with the unknown source(s) of this phenomenon. The study of this phenomenon has been hindered by looking at these incidents as isolated conduct that obscures the larger picture. Each incident can be dismissed as an aberration when looking at it in isolation. Limiting the scope of study can result in missed opportunities to learn how to cope with these rare experiences.

Former defense official Christopher Mellon recently wrote in a *Washington Post* opinion piece that the Defense Department looks at each incident separately. He wrote:

"… I know from numerous discussions with Pentagon officials over the past two years that military departments and agencies treat such incidents as isolated events rather than as part of a pattern requiring serious attention and investigation."[69]

Taking each encounter in isolation, one can always find fault with the quality of the camera or the testimony of a witness. Yet, the same type objects keep appearing and performing the same maneuvers. This has been the story since World War II. However, each era finds officials making the same mistakes and ignoring similar past cases.

The 1964 NICAP, *The UFO Evidence,* presented Congress with much of the same information that current witnesses and electronic

---

69   Mellon, Christopher, "The Military Keeps Encountering UFOs. Why Doesn't the Pentagon Care?" Washington Post, March 9, 2018.

information have captured in this century. If there is no risk from the phenomenon, these patterns would be of no importance. Yet, there is a concern that this phenomenon, at minimum, is a safety risk to military personnel. High-speed passes and aerobatics around military and civilian aircraft poses a risk even if these craft mean no harm. A pilot who is unfamiliar with this phenomenon may take evasive action that could create a greater risk. Without acknowledgment and training to help our pilots respond to these rare situations, the next unfortunate accident could be caused by the wrong reaction of a good pilot experiencing something they never knew existed. The current reluctance of our military to investigate and help its pilots respond to this phenomenon could have tragic consequences.

VI

———— ⌇⌇ ————

RECOMMENDED COMMITTEE APPROACH

THE REFERRAL BY THE Senate Select Intelligence Committee, originally attached to Senate 3095 (116th Congress), is primarily concerned with the potential threat that the UFO/UAP phenomenon presents. This emphasis is a proper approach for the Armed Services and Select Intelligence Committees to take. Once the requested report is received by these four committees, it is recommended that they begin their review with the most recent three incidents with declassified footage of each encounter. It is likely that the members who have been briefed about these incidents have seen footage that is far superior to that released to the public. Even enhanced footage does not provide Congress with the full picture of the implications of these incidents. Congress will need to overcome its historic reluctance to conduct oversight of government operations addressing this phenomenon. Unless it conducts hearings that help educate itself before taking any action, Congress will not know whether actions it takes will address the issue appropriately.

If the past is prologue, Congress will rubberstamp any policy brought to it by the defense and intelligence community. A brief review of congressional deference to the military's handling of the UFO/UAP issue is instructive. Since Senator Richard Russell's 1955 deference to the request of the Air Force to keep quiet about the issue, attempts to bring forward a serious discussion of the UFO/UAP issue have been largely thwarted by the military. In January 1958, Senator John McClellan (D-Ark.) inquired about having Government Operations Subcommittee conduct hearings. The Air Force pushed back, claimed there was no reason to hold hearings. The fact that hearings were held would create "uncontrolled publicity."[70] No hearings were held.

Uncontrolled publicity is what the Air Force and the CIA were trying to prevent during this early period of the phenomenon. The CIA, after the classified 1953 Robertson Panel, lamented the publication of books about flying saucers.[71] The panel report recommended that witnesses should be "debunked" and organizations who study the phenomenon should be placed under surveillance.[72] Air Force regulations were also implemented to prevent commercial pilots from talking about their sightings.[73] While trying to curtail speech about the subject, the Air Force conducted a public relations campaign to "debunk" UFO/UAPs.[74]

The CIA Robertson Panel claimed that the public would fall prey to "mass hysteria." This unsubstantiated claim that UFO/UAPs would cause panic is a familiar trope. The actions that were taken after the Robertson Panel amounted to suppression of speech of those who studied the phenomenon and UFO/UAP groups needed to be "watched." In the cold war climate, Congress deferred to the Air Force without public debate. During this time, Representative John E. Henderson (R-Ohio) sent written questions to the Air Force about the phenomenon. In

---

70   Jacobs, David, UFO Controversy in America, Signet Books (1975), p. 141.
71   https://jplufo.com/wp-content/uploads/2021/01/DOC_0005515979.pdf (https://www.cia.gov/library/readingroom/docs/DOC_0005515979.pdf).
72   Report Of Scientific Advisory Panel On Unidentified Flying Objects Convened By Office Of Scientific Intelligence, CIA. January 14–18, 1953, Tab "A", January 17, 1953; http://www.cufon.org/cufon/robert.htm ("Robertson Panel" or "Durant Report").
73   http://project1947.com/fig/1954a.htm A Scripps-Howard news service reports of February 13, 1954 stated, in part, that: "Airline pilots are asked not to discuss their sightings publicly or give them to newspapers."
74   Jacobs, David, UFO Controversy in America, Signet Books (1975), p. 154–159.

response, the Air Force briefed Henderson and several other congressmen about the subject. Parts of the classified Robertson Panel Report were distributed, likely without the Robertson Panel Report language about suppression of speech. Declassified records show that portions about speech limitations were left out of versions of the Robertson Panel Report sent out to some agencies in 1953. It can be reasonably assumed that the language limiting speech was left out of the versions given to members of Congress in the 1958 briefing.

Even members of Congress who were part of leadership could not hold hearings about the subject. House Majority Leader John McCormick (D-Mass.) requested UFO/UAP hearings later in the Summer of 1958. However, after a presentation by Air Force officials, no witnesses were called. This trend continued into the 1965–1967 wave of sightings. Then House Majority Leader John McCormick and House Minority Leader Gerald Ford were among those who advocated oversight hearings after sightings again dominated the headlines. Only one short hearing, labeled a "symposium," was held on July 29, 1968. Otherwise, congressional efforts have been limited to cryptic Air Force briefings or outright refusals to participate in open congressional oversight hearings.

By the 1990s, more calls came for hearings after claims of a coverup of a crash in Roswell, New Mexico became an overnight sensation. Congressmember Steve Schiff (R-NM) called for hearings. Instead the Air Force put out two studies at a cost of $40,000,000 that added a third and fourth Air Force explanation of what caused the "crash" in the New Mexico desert. No hearings were held to review either of the two Air Force reports.

Overall, the pattern is consistent. The Defense Department has aggressively fought any attempt for Congress to review the government's policy about UFO/UAPs. It has been reported that in 2019 some members of Congress have had briefings with personnel, chosen by the Defense Department.[75] However, the public record still shows that Congress has never heard from an independent witness to a UFO/UAP event in a setting that isn't controlled by the Defense Department.

Throughout history, the armed forces have had trained observers witness these events. Most of these witnesses monitored sightings using some form of electronic data collection. Yet, the electronic data of these incidents routinely disappear. The pattern is repeated with each event and nothing is learned that can help service personnel cope with these events. Frontline military personnel are deliberately kept in the dark about the phenomenon that, at a minimum, could constitute a safety hazard. At worst, they constitute a threat from an adversary. This strategy of hiding information from frontline military personnel has been consistent since World War II.

By 2020, this strategy began to unravel. The Defense Department went from January's refusal to turn over the three Navy videos because to do so would be a "grave danger to national security" to partial declassification of the videos in April. In May, the Defense Department admitted the existence of the Navy's UAP Task Force. By August, in response to the Senate Intel's request for a report, the Defense Department appointed its number two person, Deputy Defense Secretary David Norquist, to oversee the Naval UAP Task Force. The question is whether this move was intended to help or hinder transparency about the task force's work. Which course of action the new administration will take is unknown. It is up to the four committees, slated to receive the UAP Task Force report, to determine whether they break precedent with the past "hands-off" approach of Congress. Congress should independently decide which witnesses to call and what data to review.

NIMITZ CARRIER GROUP REVIEW

The release of the videos that have been shown to some members of Congress gives the four committees a good starting point. Each

---

75   https://www.politico.com/story/2019/06/19/warner-classified-briefing-ufos-1544273

committee can look into the phenomenon and determine how they impact defense readiness and/or pose a threat to national security. While the public versions of these videos have a grainy quality, the classified versions should give better insight into the objects' unique capabilities. The Nimitz Carrier Group video provides the best available information for several reasons. Because it is the earliest of the three videos, the 2004 Nimitz incidents provide an initial marker for Congress to consider how long the potential threat has been in existence.[76]

In addition to the videos, the committees have multiple, trained witnesses that can attest to the capabilities of the objects and to how the Navy reacted to them. As shown in the last section, the performance characteristics for craft in three declassified videos (2004–2015) raise serious questions about the ability of our current defenses to oppose these objects if hostile. If hostile, there is a need to change the Defense Department's 73-year policy that UFOs do not constitute a threat to national security. However, determining hostility will require more information than three grainy videos can provide. Determining the intent and the identity of the controllers of these objects will require a review of all available information gathered by human and national technical means.

As shown in Section V, using the 2004 Nimitz Carrier Group sightings as a starting point, a wealth of information has been preserved from these incidents.[77] Statements by crew members indicate that non-military personnel arrived on scene immediately and obtained electronic data about the incident from the U.S.S. Nimitz and U.S.S. Princeton. Once the agency holding this information is identified by Congress, it should be readily available to the committees in a classified setting. In addition, the pilots, commanding officers, and

---

76   As discussed previously, the existence of this phenomenon and its interactions goes back to World War II. However, the Nimitz Carrier Group incidents are the first known UFO/UAP reports that have modern electronic data, corroborated by highly trained witness testimony that is available to Congress.

77   As discussed below, the 2004 Nimitz Carrier Group sightings raise questions about the origins of the UAPs.

radar personnel are available as witnesses, many of whom have already made public statements about the series of incidents that caused the cancellation of a training exercise. Some witnesses are still bound by security oaths and cannot publicly discuss their experiences. Even if the conduct of the objects was benign, the interference with a training exercise for a carrier group getting ready to deploy for combat support operations is significant. It affects Navy readiness. Even if the multiple objects were not a threat, the origin of the objects needs to be determined to prevent interference in naval operations.

Electronic data should be obtained from other agencies that might identify where the UFO/UAPs originated. Since testimony shows that data was removed from the Nimitz Carrier Group, it is reasonable to assume similar data from other sources was also retained. This information would help the Armed Services and Select Intelligence Committees understand the potential threat, if any, to naval operations. Those agencies that provide electronic intelligence to our armed forces could provide early warning to help the military prepare for future incidents. Whether the UFO/UAPs are a direct threat or merely a navigation hazard, a coordinated identification effort must provide as early of a warning as possible.

Active and retired personnel witnessed these events and could provide testimony about the performance characteristics of the unknown craft. They could also discuss the reactions of naval personnel to the objects. This would help the armed services committees determine what kind of training programs should be funded to address these incursions. The quick identification and appropriate response can be more likely if our forces are trained and prepared for these eventualities. Keeping them in the dark about the phenomenon could lead to unintended outcomes. An unprepared military raises the chances of interactions that could lead to loss of life. Protection of our service personnel should override any other priority.

The publicly available articles and interviews provide valuable information about the objects seen in the three videos. They are able to maneuver at speeds well beyond human and aircraft endurance limits. Even when exceeding the sound barrier, there were no sonic booms normally associated with conventional aircraft. There were no air disturbances created by any of the objects. Despite their exceptional performance characteristics, none of the craft demonstrated any visible means of propulsion.

The radar on the U.S.S. Princeton, an Aegis Cruiser, witnessed a drop in altitude by the objects from 80,000 to 28,000 feet in 0.75 seconds. The change in altitude was corroborated by multiple radar returns from other ships in the Nimitz Carrier Group. This rapid change in altitude far exceeds our technical capabilities. This data was later collected by personnel with apparent authority to override standard naval procedures. The location of this electronic data is not known. Also, one of the craft exhibited the ability to accelerate instantaneously to incredible speeds that, in a conventional craft, would crush the pilot from the g-forces. This maneuver was witnessed by a wing commander and Naval Academy graduate.

The 2004 Nimitz Carrier Group incidents highlight the importance of our electronic surveillance equipment. Assuming that the series of November 2004 incidents were the first recorded by naval forces, what upgrades in the systems occurred before the objects registered in the Aegis combat information center on board the U.S.S. Princeton? The type of system improvements could hold a clue to detection of these objects in the future.[78] Assuming that the objects are determined to be a threat, the types of improvements in our electronic detection equipment could hold the key to earlier detection of these objects.

During one encounter, one pilot claimed that he could not achieve "lock-on" of his onboard weapons system. Even though there was no indication of jamming, the weapons on board his fighter aircraft would not hold a lock on the UFO/UAP. Information provided by the pilot could assist in determining the cause of this weapons failure.

---

78   https://www.politico.com/magazine/story/2017/12/16/pentagon-ufo-search-harry-reid-216111

The inability to achieve "lock-on" by weapons systems on our fighter aircraft means that the carrier group was defenseless. It is likely that the electronic data will yield information that might detect how this occurs.

One of the most disturbing elements about the Nimitz encounters is the object's foreknowledge of the combat air patrol (CAP) point. Before one of the pilots returned to his station, the object disengaged from its maneuvers near the pilot's fighter aircraft. It flew to the CAP point ahead of the pilot. When he arrived, the same craft was already at the CAP point.

Since information about the location of a CAP point is classified, how did the craft know about its location? By some unknown means, the craft learned about classified information stored in a secure system. The implications of this development are staggering. Assuming the UFO/UAPs posed a threat, the plans and operational data of a carrier group may have been freely available to this potential adversary. It was available during an engagement with a potentially hostile force that possesses far-superior technology. This 2004 revelation raises questions about whether countermeasures have been developed in the intervening 16 years. If not, what plans does the Defense Department have to remedy the issue?

The unknown craft also performed other maneuvers beyond the capability of our planes. When a group of them were cruising at 80,000 feet, it was at a speed of 100 knots. Conventional aircraft would stall flying at this speed and altitude. When the Nimitz Carrier Group testimony is compared to information derived from a 2013 Coast Guard incident, there is the intriguing possibility that the craft can move as fast underwater as in the air.[79] This video shows a small object travel at the same rate of speed above and below the waterline. In the Nimitz Carrier Group reports, one Navy pilot observed turbulence in the water, just underneath a "tic tac" object that hovered above the disturbance.

---

79   The Black Vault: https://www.youtube.com/watch?v=PJpyJ_G9WVA.

If the turbulence were caused by one of these 40-foot-wide "tic tacs," it would mean that the objects have "transmedium" capabilities and can move under the water, as well as in the air.

QUESTIONS FOR THE COMMITTEES

The four committees will assess whether these objects constitute a threat to the United States. If it is a threat, who is behind the threatening conduct? Even if the objects are not a threat, do they pose a navigational threat to the Navy during its operations?

The original request asked for recommendations of funding and programmatic adjustments to meet the concern. Based on the aftermath of these three groups of incidents, Congress should also look at post-incident procedures to determine if policy adjustments need to be made. Based on non-classified evidence, past and present, there is apparently no follow-up or after-action efforts to assist frontline personnel in anticipating and reacting to the UFO/UAP phenomenon. Post-Nimitz encounters, the electronic records from the multiple encounters were taken from the carrier group. There were no after-action reports or any official discussion to determine better ways of dealing with the phenomenon. Nothing could be learned from the incidents because, except for typical ship scuttlebutt, there was no recognition that these incidents ever took place. The question becomes, if there was a threat from these objects, why wouldn't there be an effort to learn from the incidents and help other naval personnel.[80] Congressional inquiries should try to determine if there is a policy that fails to deal with potential threats or navigation hazards that needs to be reconsidered.

---

80   The lack of follow up with personnel in the Nimitz Carrier Group post-incidents is part of a historical pattern. For the length of the phenomenon, the same pattern emerges. An unidentified object is spotted near U.S. military forces. Post-incident, service personnel are not to speak of the incident. All data that documents the incident is removed from the units involved. There is no after-action consultation, and the incident is hushed up. (See, generally: Salas, Robert & Klotz, James, Faded Giant, BookSurge, LLC (2005); Hastings, Robert, UFOs and Nukes: Extraordinary Encounters at Nuclear Weapons Sites, AuthorHouse (2008); Pope, Nick et. al., Encounter in Rendlesham Forest, Thomas Dunne Books (2014); Lovelace, Terry, Incident at Devils Den, Kindle Direct Publishing (2018).)

General questions about the UFO/UAP phenomenon should include the following inquiries:

a. Should the committees consider legislation and appropriations that supports training to prepare for potential engagements with UFO/UAPs? Whether a direct threat or a potential navigation hazard, what policy changes should be made to help readiness of land, sea, air, and space assets?

The four committees will have to determine whether there is a need for legislation to address some impediment to understanding the UFO/UAP phenomenon. It could be removal of an artificial separation of data, personnel, or programs that could help better understand the phenomenon if those barriers were lowered. There could be funding recommended to emphasize countermeasures in the annual appropriations legislation. Overall, the committees will be deciding if the report addressed the issues contained in the referral. If there are still questions that were not answered, the committees will need to require follow-up inquiries.

Any legislative proposal should include language that congressional leadership be kept apprised of the progress of these programs regardless of their security classification. At a minimum, elected leadership in the Congress and the executive branch should be frequently briefed on program progress.

b. Should the committees consider legislation and appropriations to conduct research into countermeasures if any aspect of the phenomena is officially deemed a threat?

If the committees are given credible information that shows a terrestrial threat exists, all methods of meeting that threat must be considered. Since these discussions would take place in a classified setting, there is little a private citizen can do to understand the steps that need to be taken. However, a majority of Americans believe that the United States government is hiding knowledge of UFO/UAPs. Great care must be taken to make sure that there is specific evidence to justify a "terrestrial threat" determination. Regardless of the origin of the threat, there will need to be some public justification that assures the American people that their elected representatives are making the decisions in the public's best interest. Vague claims that a non-specific threat exists that needs to be dealt with cannot be the basis of legislation. The trust factor has a very thin margin given past history of the government's *de facto* policy that UFO/UAPs do not exist.

    c.   What resources, if any, should be expended to determine if a hostile nation is in possession of the crafts that have been observed by U.S. forces?

Obviously, on proof that a terrestrial adversary possesses operational versions of this technology, Congress must act to respond to the threat. The cost and types of programs should contain the legislative language discussed under (a), above.

    d.   Should the committees consider legislation and appropriations to assist in the coordination of programs to develop similar technology for civilian and military use?

The need for appropriations to develop similar technology is apparent. The type of research and the accountability of these programs to our elected representatives should require legislation to ensure oversight. Without oversight, the progress and costs of any programs existing or to be established will be uncontrolled. While secrecy should surround any cutting-edge defense research, some form of oversight will be required. Also, safeguards should be put in place to prevent potential leaps in technology from being of military benefit only. Civilian and other governmental applications should be made available and protected by legislation.

    e.   Should the committees consider legislation and appropriations that establishes the criteria for determining if this phenomena is a threat to U.S. forces and territory?

A key question will be how Congress determines the degree of risk from these objects to our homeland. This will be a long-term issue that should not be hastily arrived at during initial hearings after the report is issued to the four committees. Unless the report sets out clearly defined evidence of a known terrestrial threat, the congressional committees must be ready to pursue more information to give itself some sense of the import of these UFO/UAP incidents. New efforts for gathering evidence of past (pre-2004) incidents can assist Congress in unraveling the mystery.

How Congress Should Define a "Threat"

These general questions hinge on another question. Congress also needs to better define what factors constitute a "threat." How a "threat" is defined will determine how the general questions, listed above, are answered. The "threat" determination must include specific factors that define what sort of conduct constitutes a threat. We should use the three video sightings as only a starting point. However, a larger sample size is needed. Any long-term assessment of the threat posed by this phenomenon must rely on World War II experiences forward.

The 2004 Nimitz Carrier Group incidents are typical in that they were observational appearances by the craft. The "tic tacs" mimicked the maneuvers of the fighter jets from the U.S.S. Nimitz. They also largely avoided attempts to engage by the Nimitz fighters. After displaying remarkable aerial feats, they either left the immediate area at impossible speeds or continued their slow transit towards the south, off Baja, California. They did not display any direct hostility but performed in a manner consistent with the World War II "foo fighters" and other previous military encounters. They were considered navigation hazards because of their manner of engagement and their high-performance capabilities. Yet, they were never considered more than a hazard. The 2014–2015 incidents off the East Coast involving the U.S.S. Roosevelt had largely similar behavior from different unknown craft.

Historically, many of the incidents involve the observation of military forces, especially during training/combat operations. This aspect of the UFO/UAP phenomenon has been a consistent theme since World War II. Observation at close quarters without engagement. Every decade since WWII has had similar incidents. The object will shadow a military aircraft, mimicking many maneuvers, and then quickly leave the scene. NICAP produced a congressional booklet which showed this pattern from 1942 to 1963. NICAP's *The UFO Evidence* detailed UFO sighting information through the years, including military encounters. NICAP provided Congress with helpful information concerning UFO/UAP sightings by military and civilians.

While cases demonstrated curiosity rather than hostile intent, there were also cases that raise greater security concerns. Most of these involved nuclear facilities. There have been many incursions into secure space that resulted in various degrees of tampering with our nuclear facilities, including missiles in their silos.[81] At a minimum, these reports show that UFO/UAPs have affected our readiness to launch a retaliatory nuclear strike.

An example of these disturbing incidents is the 1967 Oscar Flight, where eight of 10 intercontinental ballistic missiles (ICBM) went offline while a UFO/UAP hovered over the command silo.[82] In the early morning hours of March 16, 1967, a bright red-orange UFO hovered

---

81 Hastings, Robert, UFOs and Nukes: Extraordinary Encounters at Nuclear Weapons Sites, AuthorHouse (2008); Salas, Robert & Klotz, James, Faded Giant, BookSurge, LLC (2005).
82 Salas, Robert & Klotz, James, Faded Giant, BookSurge, LLC (2005).

silently over the launch control center (LCC) that controlled a flight of 10 ICBM missiles, scattered over the Montana landscape. The above-ground security crew called down to Air Force Academy graduate Lt. Robert Salas, who was one of the two launch officers in the below ground LCC capsule. Upon hearing the excited security officer explain what he was seeing, Lt. Salas assumed that the normally professional security crew was playing a practical joke on him. However, when missiles in Oscar Flight began going off-line, Salas took the matter seriously. Launch officers Lt. Salas and Lt. Fred Meiwald determined that there was a guidance & control system malfunction, even though power had not been shut off.

When the two-person command crew returned to Malmstrom Air Force Base, they discussed the incident with the base commander. They were told not to discuss the incident with anyone. Later, technicians from the Boeing Company arrived on scene to determine the cause of the fault. They had no explanation for the failure. Except for briefing the base commander, the two launch officers never were debriefed by anyone about the incident. While talking to a security officer on duty that shift, Lt. Robert Salas was told that Echo Flight had the same experience with its missiles going off-line while a UFO/UAP hovered nearby.

These incidents were not the only ones where a UFO/UAP caused a nuclear-tipped ICBM to go off-line. In *UFOs and Nukes: Extraordinary Encounters at Nuclear Weapons Sites* (2008) and *Faded Giant* (2005), numerous incidents are discussed where nuclear missiles are taken off-line by UFO/UAPs. Post-Soviet Union records reveal that the same incidents occurred to missiles in the U.S.S.R. According to Robert Hastings in his book *UFOs and Nukes*, these incidents have been occurring as long as the United States has had nuclear ICBMs. It is still likely to be occurring.

The method of disarming an ICBM is similar to the 2004 Nimitz Carrier Group incident where a fighter pilot was unable to achieve missile "lock-on" an unidentified 40-foot-wide flying "tic tac." Electronic interference methods are used to disable weapons of all types. These craft are able to interfere with any electronic system that controls weapons, while leaving other electronic systems operational. Our modern "fly by wire" aircraft appear to be unable to use their weapons systems against these craft. This contrasts with the "foo fighter" cases where manual machine guns in WWII bombers were able to fire their weapons, albeit with no impact on the bright balls of light.

These pre-2004 incidents show the ability of UFO/UAPs to disarm military assets. Whether these incidents are a self-defense mechanism, or an offensive threat, is unknown. Each committee will need to get answers to the questions surrounding incidents that appear to be consistent for 70-plus years.

With the appropriate information in hand, the "threat" determination must consider what level of conduct should be considered a military threat. If the observational and limited engagements demonstrated in the three videos are a product of a domestic adversary, it is likely that these actions are intended to prepare them for a future conflict. Any terrestrial country that would engage a potential foreign adversary in this manner is getting ready for conflict. If there is a terrestrial threat, the actions towards the Nimitz and Roosevelt Carrier Groups foretell possible preparation for a conflict. It would seem that a potential conflict would also be more likely if the adversary had a newly acquired technological advantage. Focusing on these 21ˢᵗ century incidents, there would certainly be alarm with unknown craft conducting surveillance of our military assets.

Yet, viewing these three incidents in isolation would require us to artificially limit the data in a way that could skew the result towards a high threat risk. Yet, this behavior is so similar to past incidents dating back to World War II. Looking at the conduct of these objects over a longer period would lessen the chances that the behavior foretells a future armed conflict. In order to assess the threat risk, Congress will need more data to determine what conduct has been occurring in the long-term and what actions are of recent vintage. Are the 2004–2015 carrier group incidents unique or are they merely recent incidents with the same signature?

What information is brought forward by the DNI and SecDef could affect the bottom-line threat determination. As with the 1953 Robertson Panel review, limiting the amount of relevant data can change the outcome of Congress's analysis. The more the recent events look like past events dating back to World War II, the less likelihood that we are facing a terrestrial threat.

In the absence of a terrestrial explanation for this phenomenon, the activities undertaken by the intelligence(s) behind it may not be for a sinister purpose. Their interest in our nuclear weapons may be defensive in nature. If so, our first step should not assume the conduct is intended to be aggressive. Without a record of aggressive incidents that these craft have taken over the last 70-plus years, it is unlikely that the intelligences behind these incidents are an existential threat. The question becomes how much information about past interactions is the DNI and SecDef willing to share with Congress. The less information they share about pre-2004 UFO/UAP conduct, the less likely that we are dealing with a threat.

Basic social science tells us that group decisions are less likely to be successful if some participants in the decision-making process have access to more information that is not shared with the entire group.[83] Without a comparison between 21st century incidents and past conduct, the decisions Congress makes will have a higher probability of failure. Based on publicly known information, this phenomenon has not exhibited overtly aggressive behavior towards our military over the last 70-plus years. The classified record may tell a different story. Regardless of what the past record of UFO/UAP interactions entails, this information is vital to help Congress set broad legislative policy that is based on all available evidence.

A "threat analysis" must consider the length that this observational

---

83   Stangor, Dr. Charles, Jhangiani, Dr. Rajiv, & Tarry, Dr. Hammond, Principles of Social Psychology - 1st International Edition, BCC Campus, p. 481 et. seq. (Ch. 10 Group Decision-Making).

behavior has been occurring. It must also include an analysis of whether any aggressive actions have occurred when our weapons systems have been deactivated. What other aggressive actions have taken place that have had a negative effect on our force readiness. Congress needs to know what conduct has been occurring for decades. For example, one of the earliest NATO military exercises experienced similar observational conduct.[84] NATO's largest early naval exercise, Operation Mainbrace, attracted multiple UFO/UAPs that reconnoitered the September 1952 operations in the Baltic Sea and North Atlantic. However, there is no record of these objects engaged in aggressive behavior. Unless the classified record identifies specific acts of aggression taken by non-terrestrial actors, the risk possibilities are much lower if the only source of the UFO/UAP is off-planet rather than a terrestrial source.

This presumption is based on the demonstrated record of our terrestrial adversaries and their motives versus the lack of overt actions of war-like aggression taken by UFO/UAPs over time. One thing is clear, the UFO/UAP phenomenon is so technologically advanced that the intelligence(s) behind this phenomenon have the capability of acting aggressively towards our military. The question becomes whether this capability is coupled with an intent to harm. The answer to this question, based on currently available information, is that aggressive intentions are unlikely present.

Consider that this phenomenon has been around at least since World War II. Its actions do indicate a special interest in nuclear power, both peaceful and military uses.[85] Besides acts of observation and some short-term weapons system interference, there are no instances of UFO/UAPs taking unilateral aggressive actions. United States forces have not been attacked by these objects to date. Unless this premise is contradicted by classified evidence, UFO/UAPs do not pose an

---

84 National Investigations Committee on Aerial Phenomenon (NICAP), Richard H. Hall (Editor), The UFO Evidence (1964), reprint Barnes & Noble Books (1997), pp. 162–163.
85 See, generally: Salas, Robert & Klotz, James, Faded Giant, BookSurge, LLC (2005); Hastings, Robert, UFOs and Nukes: Extraordinary Encounters at Nuclear Weapons Sites, AuthorHouse (2008); Pope, Nick et. al., Encounter in Rendlesham Forest, Thomas Dunne Books (2014).

immediate threat to our military through affirmative acts of aggression. While past actions do not guarantee future conduct, the lack of a terrestrial threat lowers the risk of UFO/UAPs attacking our military.

Threat analysis should not be defined solely by capability. The United States is capable of aggressive conduct to settle foreign policy disputes. But in the vast majority of situations, the U.S. has resorted to diplomatic measures to respond to inappropriate conduct. Given the 70-year-plus track record of non-aggression, a military-first response to the phenomenon should not be our policy. A "threat" finding should be based on capabilities plus overt aggressive actions taken. Our terrestrial adversaries, China and Russia, meet this threshold. The unknown non-terrestrial sources, if any, do not meet this threshold without more evidence of aggressive conduct.

VII

PUBLIC POLICY CHANGES
TO ASSIST OVERSIGHT

THE FOUR COMMITTEES WILL need to decide whether the materials in the report about the UFO/UAP phenomenon contain enough information to make the proper public policy decisions. If not, other measures need to be taken to shed light on the subject. There are a number of public policy changes that could help Congress gain a more complete picture about the UFO/UAP phenomenon. They would assist elected public officials in setting a course towards understanding. For over 70-plus years, decision-making has been left to the unelected. Policy changes require evidence. Congressional officials cannot act without having the facts at their disposal.

Under the Freedom of Information Act (FOIA), UFO-related documents are hidden from public view usually for two reasons. They are withheld because releasing the document would compromise "national security" or would compromise the "sources and methods" used in intelligence collection. Either through a presidential executive order or congressional legislation, the declassification process must be streamlined, and the presumptions in these incidents should be weighted towards disclosure. For documents, photographs, and other evidence that are still classified, this information should be provided to the appropriate congressional committees for review in a classified setting. Congressional leaders with appropriate security clearances were informed of the Osama bin Laden raid before it occurred. Shouldn't they be allowed to see what is being hidden from the public about UFO/UAPs? There have been too many stories of federal elected representatives being unable to access this information from the military over the years. House Minority Leader, Warren Commission member and future President Gerald Ford, New Mexico Congressman Steven Schiff and Arizona Senator Barry Goldwater are among many who have been rebuffed when looking for information about the UFO phenomenon.

The first area of needed reform deals with the classified record. For a phenomenon that the government says does not exist, there is a high degree of classification. Even with declassified documents, it takes 55-plus years to allow the public to see them. At this rate, the public will find out what happened on the U.S.S. Nimitz off the coast of San Diego in 2004 no sooner than 2059. After the December 2017 *New York Times* article showing a blurry tic tac-shaped object through a fighter jet's gun camera, the Pentagon decided not to release any further information because of national security concerns. For example, in a letter dated January 27, 2020, John Greenewald (*Black Vault,* a private government document repository) was denied materials he requested about the 2004 Nimitz incident because of national security concerns. The later reversal allowed the three incidents to be revealed but there are still 70-plus years of incidents to be reviewed.

Even declassified documents from the 1940s and 1950s still obscure the names of long dead CIA personnel who were involved. The only plausible reason is to prevent the public from knowing who was involved. The names of many of the principals on the distribution lists are declassified. However, the staff making presentations about the phenomenon are still protected in most instances.

The "national security" exception needs to be changed to declassify information about a phenomenon that is officially not a threat. Unless something is a threat, records should never be withheld under this exception. If something seen in the sky is not a terrestrial foreign military asset, it should not be classified. Hiding behind "national security" prevents Congress and the public from jointly discussing the implications of the UFO/UAP phenomenon.

The FOIA restriction of "sources" is also overly broad when it comes to UFO/UAP incidents. The exemption for "sources" is meant to protect the identities of personnel involved in espionage or classified programs. Most pilots who take gun camera footage are not part of a classified program. Most photos of UFOs are taken by people being in the right place at the precise time. The same is likely true of most military photographs containing UFO/UAPs. For instance, if a sailor on ship watch had taken a picture of the unusual object that was mentioned in the ship log, the photo should be available to Congress. At a minimum, photographs like this should be made available to our congressional representatives either in a classified or public setting.

Under the "methods" in the intelligence gathering exception, there should be a specific policy that prevents use of this exception to protect technological methods already in the public domain. An example is satellite photography no more accurate than Google Earth technology. It should be publicly available. Classified data collection methods using current cutting-edge technology should still be protected. However, most information is not collected through a classified method. Most UFO sightings likely held in government records are generated domestically with no use of clandestine human sources or sophisticated technology unknown to our terrestrial enemies. The fact that a photograph is taken in the United States makes it highly unlikely that the source is classified. Any photos taken domestically should be presumed to be available to the public. Photos taken on military bases can redact classified equipment or facilities. Gun camera footage should be available. It is always available to the public when the government wants to show the "shock and awe" of a military campaign, yet it is classified if it shows a UFO/UAP. Any photos taken by NASA should be fair game for the public to review without areas blanked out. In the 1960s, the military worked with NASA to take high-resolution photos of the dark side on the Moon. Yet, the unredacted, high resolution photos are still not available. While there may be nothing unusual on the far side of the Moon, the failure to allow high-quality, unredacted photos of the mapping survey invite speculation. If there is nothing to see in space or on the Moon, why are we still protecting photos that were taken using technology that included film and vacuum tube computers?

Formerly classified methods should have an automatic shelf life that presumes the technology no longer needs to be protected after 20 years. Either by executive order or congressional legislation, a time limit should be placed on use of this exception unless the head of the responsible federal agency certifies, by clear and convincing evidence, that the technology still needs to be protected. Military secrets involving nuclear weapon technology, stealth technology and other similar military secrets would easily retain their protection under this policy. Documents, especially photographic materials, are still being withheld from the distant past when the technical means were far less superior than today. Formerly classified methods should have an automatic shelf life that does not exceed 20 years unless there is a factual justification presented to the agency head that the need to remain classified is shown.

SECURITY OATHS

A second area of concern involves security oaths. Many military and civilian personnel are sworn to secrecy after witnessing a UFO. In 1986, a Federal Aviation Administration accident investigator watched a group of federal civilian employees being sworn to secrecy by CIA officials about a UFO/UAP air incident over Alaskan airspace.[86] Forty-

---

86   Hastings, Robert, UFOs and Nukes: Extraordinary Encounters at Nuclear Weapons Sites, AuthorHouse (2008), pp. 185–186. http://www.ufohastings.com/

four years later, none of these federal employees can speak about the incident. Through a bureaucratic error, former FAA accident investigator John Callahan never signed the same secrecy oath. Because of the lifetime security oaths, he had no independent witnesses to verify his claim. Lifetime security oaths should not be the norm, they should be the rare exception since most military personnel serve while they are young adults and lifetime restrictions are particularly burdensome on the free speech rights of veterans.

Balancing the need for secrecy with the rights of people to discuss matters of public concern must be addressed. Except for government personnel that are bound by secrecy from a classified program which they voluntarily joined, there should be a time limit on security oaths. A change, by legislation or executive order, could limit the duration of a security oath to 20 years unless circumstances show that there is a demonstrated need to prolong it. The continuation of a security oath could be controlled through legislation or administrative action. For instance, when Congress appropriates funds for a classified program, the legislation could include a provision that sets up the time limits on secrecy. Certain programs could allow for a lifetime secrecy oath in the case of nuclear weapons development, biological warfare, and similar large-risk programs. However, personnel who are not part of a classified program but are asked to sign security oaths should have their oaths limited to 20 years absent extraordinary circumstances. These extraordinary circumstances should be factually and legally sufficient to outweigh their free speech rights. After 20 years, a security oath that is not part of a classified program should be null and void. If the federal government wishes to extend the secrecy beyond its original life span, it can notify the oath taker, either personally or via a post on a government website. The person could check the status in this way and file an administrative appeal if they believe the extension unduly interferes with free speech rights.

Setting up an administrative appeal process would be simple. The federal government has hundreds of these types of administrative procedures across the entire range of government. A review would balance the need for secrecy versus the free speech rights of the oath taker. At the end of the administrative process, an aggrieved party could challenge the agency's determination in court.

Time limitations would help the typical witness to a UFO/UAP sighting be able to eventually talk about it. If a sailor sees a UFO/UAP fly over a ship that she is stationed on, she could talk about it after enough time has passed. If the object turns out to be a secret weapon, the secrecy period could logically be extended. A generic response could be given to the person who wants the secrecy lifted so as not to give clues away as to the specific reason for the secrecy. If the person does not agree with the administrative determination, they could seek judicial review. Classified information that is still sensitive could be revealed *in camera* in the judge's chambers to protect its secrecy. The person would have their day in court, protecting their free speech rights. If the court finds that the oath was wrongfully restricted, methods could be built in to award attorney's fees to the prevailing citizen whose rights were illegally restricted. An award mechanism would give the government a disincentive to continue improper speech restrictions.

WITNESS PROTECTION

A third area of reform would be protections for people who come forward with unusual evidence. While there is no longer an Air Force program to investigate UFO/UAPs, the military still comments on sightings that attract attention of the media. Several past cases show examples of people who were branded as hoaxers by the Air Force without recourse for the damage to their reputations. If the Pentagon investigates an incident and brands a person as a hoaxer, there should be an administrative recourse for the person to present evidence to protect their reputations. Name-clearing hearings are commonly allowed in a variety of contexts by governmental agencies. Most states have a public name-clearing hearing process for persons whose reputations have been damaged by a government action. With minimal procedures, the aggrieved person has a public forum to contest the government's adverse action that damages their reputation.

WHISTLEBLOWER PROTECTIONS

In addition to procedural protections, the federal government needs to give Congress better access to information about the phenomenon. In the past, there have been numerous incidents where elected officials have been rebuffed in their attempts to discover information about the UFO phenomenon. While information will be found in classified special access programs, security clearances can be given to designated elected representatives who have oversight responsibility. The question becomes where to look for the information. As with many "black budget" programs, oversight is a difficult process. In the past, there have been numerous instances where it is difficult to determine who is in charge of the program at issue. As shown by the 1970s Senate "Church" Committee, fake identifications, clandestine activities, and other nefarious means make it difficult to determine who is involved.[87]

With subterfuge that is documented in declassified records, it would be highly suspect if Congress were told that there is nothing more to see. If there was evidence of the UFO phenomenon in the depths of government or with government contractors, it would be difficult to track down without the help of someone who has knowledge of where the information is located. A congressional committee cannot issue a subpoena if you do not know who to send it to. Congress could use an established procedure that allows grievances against the government to help them find information hidden from Congress.

A traditional method of learning about wrongdoing, waste, or fraud in government is through a whistleblower program. All federal

---

87   Church Committee (U.S. Senate Select Committee on Intelligence Activities Within the United States), Intelligence Activities and the Rights of Americans: 1976 U.S. Senate Report on Illegal Wiretaps and Domestic Spying by the FBI, CIA and NSA (2007), Red and Black Publishers.

agencies have a whistleblower procedure for employees and contractors to use. It gives persons who are aware of wrongdoing an outlet to inform policymakers of waste, fraud, and abuse in the system. This existing program could be used to find out if our tax dollars are used to hide things from Congress and the public about the UFO/UAP phenomenon. Even for sensitive matters, the intelligence agencies use whistleblower programs to disclose wrongdoing. For serious complaints, the inspector general is required to submit the report of a whistleblower within seven days to the House and Senate Select Intelligence and/or Armed Services Committees. Non-urgent complaints are submitted as part of a routine process on a semi-annual basis.

The existing whistleblower process could be used to allow current and former employees or contractors to submit information about the government's involvement in the UFO/UAP phenomenon that might assist Congress in gaining information about this subject. This can be accomplished through either new legislation that amends the process or possibly an executive order which sets up the ability of current and former personnel to submit information about the UFO/UAP phenomenon to their agency's inspector general. This would give people with key information a method to inform agency heads and congressional representatives about the UFO/UAP phenomenon. The handling of each complaint would be protected from public scrutiny to prevent other classified information from being exposed. Under the current system, nothing would prevent a whistleblower from directly contacting the congressional personnel who are properly cleared to receive the information if the agency's inspector general fails to submit the information required to be submitted.

Specifically identifying this type of information, as fitting under the complaint procedures, would give comfort to a potential whistleblower. Even if they have signed a secrecy oath, they can still use the whistleblower complaint process. It is the best way to ensure that the complaint will be considered for oversight purposes. However, congressional legislation may be needed which adds this category of waste, abuse, and fraud to the whistleblower parameters. It would use an existing process that is designed to protect the complainant. While there is the chance that persons will file a speculative or false claim, the federal government has laws that make false claims a crime.

Even with these procedures, Congress may not get the information that is needed to determine whether an unconstitutional clandestine policy still exists. Assuming there are such programs, the participants may have potential liability for acts they have committed in furtherance of an active measure's "debunking" policy. Either civil or criminal liability may attach to a person coming forward to expose past improper conduct. For that reason, a program seeking witnesses to improper conduct would require an amnesty window that would give the whistleblower the confidence to come forward without retribution.

Such programs have been successful in the past. One of the biggest amnesty programs was approved administratively by President Gerald Ford. On September 16, 1974, he approved a proclamation that gave amnesty to those young men who avoided the draft during the Viet Nam War. There were conditions attached that had to be met to qualify for the immunity program. Today, a similar program could be put in place. It is recommended that any amnesty have a time limit to give qualified people a chance to come forward but is not perpetual. A perpetual amnesty program would not be an incentive to come forward.

An amnesty period of five years would be appropriate. This length of time would give current and former employees and contractors time to see how the implementation process works. Five years would span parts of two presidential terms of office. Candidates for the highest office would have a program in place that they would have to support or oppose on the campaign trail so the public would know where they stand. Public discussion about the issue would become part of the political process. Instead of being a taboo subject, the amnesty program would be a focal point for policy discussions related to the UFO/UAP phenomenon and the people affected by it. The process could be put in place with only minor changes to existing administrative procedures.

The end of the amnesty period would be a fixed time and would encourage potential complainants to weigh the pros and cons of entering the program in a timely manner. Considering the current system where documents are usually released after about 50 years, five years would be a relatively short time.

One instructive example involved three Polaroid photographs taken in 1965 by Rex Heflin, an Orange County, California highway maintenance engineer, with no interest in UFO/UAPs.[88] After a relative had his Polaroid photos published in a local paper, military personnel from North American Aerospace Defense Command (NORAD) showed up at his doorstep.[89] Heflin had lent his photos to local military personnel a few times. He then lent them to the NORAD men. However, they weren't NORAD men. The photo originals were obtained by persons who masqueraded as military officers, using fake identifications. These clandestine actors were able to keep the photographs for over 27 years. They were returned to Heflin through mysterious circumstances. Mr. Heflin received a telephone call telling him to check his mailbox. When he did, Heflin found his missing three original photographs. These circumstances suggest that they were held by some organization for a lengthy time period. Yet, this organization had the wherewithal to track him down and return them without being discovered.

Mr. Heflin, the main witness in this matter, was a person who seems unlikely to fabricate this chain of events. First, he was never a believer in UFOs before he took the pictures. He never sought attention and did not seek out the media. They came to him. He cooperated with every government official, real or fake. He never sought remuneration for his photos. His fellow employees and supervisors held him in high regard and vouched for his honesty to military officials who inquired. In fact, he initially thought that the object was a government secret project. In the end, he gave them to a non-family member who

---

88 There are many accounts of Mr. Heflin's encounter. Likely, the most detailed account was written by Ann Druffel, an important member of NICAP, for UFO Magazine in August 2006, pp. 52–63. (www.nicap.org/Reports/Goodbye_Rex_Heflin.pdf)

89 Id.

promised to have them analyzed once technology allowed for a better analysis. He is about as credible a witness as one could find.

More than 25 years later while in retirement and dying from cancer, Mr. Heflin received a call telling him to check his mailbox. The person who made the call was likely an administrative assistant conveying information at the request of her supervisors. If she were to come forward as part of a whistleblower program, it would help confirm a link between the organization she worked for and the illegal actions it undertook. It would both confirm Mr. Heflin's account and establish the identity of the organization that was involved in the disappearance and reappearance of his photographs. Would the witness know the authority for the operation? Perhaps she would understand the scope of these activities and help Congress determine whether taxpayer funds were expended improperly.

To increase the effectiveness of the amnesty program, truthful complainants would need legal protections to prevent adverse job action and protection of vested benefits. The filing of a whistleblowing complainant should protect them from retaliation. If you have signed a secrecy oath and are worried about losing your pension benefits, you would be less likely to come forward. Basic protections given to whistleblowers must be a part of any amnesty program.

With a five-year window to file, a significant number of people would likely come forward to file a complaint. Most will be former government employees who were assigned to a classified program that dealt with the UFO phenomenon. Others may be people that were in the right place at the wrong time. They saw something extraordinary while on duty at a government facility and were required to sign a secrecy oath. Because of that oath, they cannot tell.

The vast majority of the whistleblowers will not have claims for compensation. Being released from a security oath is not a compensable injury. Reporting the activities of a program to which they were assigned could grant them immunity from criminal prosecution or civil liability arising out of their activities in the program. Even if the potential complainant has no possible liability risk, the act of explaining what you witnessed by itself serves a positive purpose. Nearly all people are concerned about how they are perceived. An amnesty program would allow people to be part of the solution rather than blamed for being part of the problem.

A UFO/UAP whistleblower amnesty program would not need to have many people to come forward to make a difference. Even if only a small number came forward, it would help Congress determine whether there is a policy issue that must be addressed. There are several possibilities as to what the results would show.

First, it could show that there is no such thing as a true UFO. It could confirm the possibility that all unidentified flying objects are either the product of a mistaken witness, a delusional one, or a deliberate hoaxer. If this outcome were to be presented after a true investigation overseen by bi-partisan congressional representatives, it would more likely be accepted by the majority of Americans. For example, this would mean that the Air Force and CIA had other motives for their actions after the Robertson Panel. One possibility is that they were so fixated on the communist menace that the concern of "mass hysteria" led to a policy of civil rights violations against a small segment of Americans. The subsequent cover-up was put in place to hide these violations.

A second possibility is that the Air Force and CIA knew that they could not adequately explain what was appearing in our skies. They used the debunking/ridicule approach to buy some time until they figured it out. Once they figured it out, they would then go to the President and Congress with the answers and ask for direction to deal with what they found. Since they have never been able to figure it out, they have done everything they can to keep their ignorance under wraps. Having never "figured it out," they have continued the same concealment and "debunking" program. This possibility would demonstrate how bureaucratic inertia can continue when there is no meaningful oversight.

Under this second scenario, the decision of whether to continue the secrecy should be put in the hands of our elected officials. After 70-plus years of secrecy, perhaps there is another way to handle our inability to figure out what is behind the UFO/UAP phenomenon. Bringing our elected representatives into the decision-making process would also reduce the possibility of continued civil rights violations against unsuspecting Americans. There would likely be aspects of our study of the UFO/UAP phenomenon that could be shared with the public.

A third scenario would be that the military and intelligence communities are aware that UFOs are of extraterrestrial or inter-dimensional origin. The cover-up and "debunking" policies were put in place to allow the military to figure out how to use information about them for the defense benefit of the United States. This scenario means that the military still has not figured out how to use what they have learned to any significant extent. Or else we would have a military flying around in flying saucers with a massive advantage in any conflict. To date, we do not appear to have a flying saucer fleet. After 70-plus years, shouldn't the decisions on when and if to disclose be made by our elected representatives? While the sheer numbers of people that have been affected are likely small, any policy that impinges on the civil rights of Americans should not stand. Our civil rights depend on the good faith of our elected leaders. Absent knowledge, they will be unable to protect those rights.

Under any possible scenario, the remedial steps recommended should help move towards identification and resolution. This conundrum of a policy has used subterfuge and illegal methods to undermine the rights of American citizens. If the UFO/UAP phenomenon is not real, ridicule should not be used as a means to eliminate the problem.[90] If the UFO/UAP phenomenon is real, the answers of how to deal with it should be put into the hands of our elected representatives. In a democratic republic, constitutional protections should be available to

---

90   See, generally: Lough, James, Threat to the Body Politic: How the CIA and Air Force Suppressed the Study of UFOs, estimated publication date, June 2021.

all. They should not be denied to those who are in the right place at the wrong time and are forever branded by their association with a phenomenon not of their making. Regardless of the merits of their arguments, people who wish to associate with others who study the phenomenon should not have their rights trampled. The Constitution does not have an exception for "stuff" the government fails to understand.

One scenario that is not considered is that a cover-up is keeping a genuine threat to mankind in the dark until the military figures out how to defend us. If this scenario were true, why would an invading force wait 70-plus years to plan a takeover. No invading force gives 70 years of warnings before invading. If there was a threat to our existence, it would already have happened.

In many respects, the UFO/UAP phenomenon is not the main issue. The main issue is how, when confronted with an unusual set of circumstances, does our adherence to democratic principles continue to be our lodestar. From the declassified record and other instructive incidents, it is probable that the military and intelligence communities have departed from the democratic protections that make this country unique among nations. Does "continued emphasis on the reporting of these phenomena ..., in these parlous times, result in a threat to the orderly functioning of the protective organs of the body politic?"[91] In the alternative, is our government stronger when it deals with larger questions out in the open? The answers to these questions define us as a nation.

The reforms recommended are modest changes. These methods will allow people to come forward in a safe and orderly manner to help Congress understand what needs to be done to remedy past mistakes and ensure that our elected representatives have proper oversight methods at their disposal. The five year amnesty program would give persons a chance to come forward and present information in a safe setting that could help our representatives sort the wheat from the chaff.

---

91   Report of Scientific Advisory Panel on Unidentified Flying Objects Convened by the Office of Scientific Intelligence, CIA. January 14–18, 1953, Tab "A", Section 3a, January 17, 1953; http://www.cufon.org/cufon/robert.htm ("Robertson Panel" or "Durant Report").

VIII

CONCLUSION

THIS BRIEFING BOOK HAS discussed several important trends involving the UFO/UAP phenomenon. Since World War II, the military has studied it, starting with the foo fighters, and continuing until the present formation of the Navy's UAP Task Force. During this time, the reports from military observers have been remarkably consistent. The unknown objects, while showing some variety, have the same flight characteristics and exhibit the same types of interactions with our military assets. They occasionally mimic the maneuvers of our military planes. When challenged by our pilots, they either quickly depart the scene or suppress our electronically controlled weapons systems. Yet, other flight functions seem unaffected.

UFO/UAPs also maintain a consistent interest in our nuclear weapons. Over the years, they have shown an ability to temporarily deactivate our nuclear weapons systems. These deactivations have also happened to our adversaries. The interference has no other known cause and cannot be explained by our defense contractors who maintain the assets. It can be presumed that this activity is still going on.

Our military responses have also been consistent. Each incident is followed up by removal of all electronic data that captured the incident. Normal rules to help us learn from these incidents are ignored. Military personnel are told not to discuss these rare incidents with anyone. There is no training regimen that prepares our military personnel for these incidents. Secrecy oaths are used to make sure that frontline personnel will continue to be uninformed and unprepared for these incidents. This raises the possibility that our own forces may be exposed to danger if an incident response goes awry. In 1948, Captain Thomas Mantell, a veteran pilot, made the rookie mistake of exceeding the altitude limits without having onboard oxygen in his effort to reach an unknown object. He lost his life as a result.

Meanwhile, Congress has been consistent in its avoidance of the subject. While many inquiries by individual members of Congress have been made, there is little to show for these efforts. Since 1955, when Senator Richard Russell refused to talk to the press at the request of the military, successive Congresses have followed this silent pattern. Congress has yet to hear about any military incident from the personnel who witnessed these rare experiences. No legislative policy is influenced by the phenomenon as Congress has been largely out of the loop for 70-plus years. It has been 65 years since Senator Russell said it was not the "right time" to talk about the phenomenon.

This reticence leaves the ultimate policy making in the hands of the Defense Department and the intelligence community. Until 2020, they have been remarkably consistent in their approach to the UFO/UAP phenomenon. The official policy of the military and intelligence communities has been that all UFO/UAP claims are made by people who are (1) mistaken, (2) hoaxing, or (3) delusional. Since the early efforts to squelch discussion of the UFO/UAP phenomenon, each military incident has had the common elements discussed above. Evidence is taken from frontline units who are then told to no longer discuss what they witnessed. For a phenomenon that is not real, much effort is put into preventing anyone from learning about these incidents.

The 2020 policy changes, whether intentional or driven by press coverage, gives Congress an opportunity to reassert its oversight authority. The Senate Select Intelligence Committee has required a report on the efforts of the Navy's UAP Task Force and related questions. The request, by itself, will not change policy. Potential changes will revolve around how much information Congress receives in the report and whether Congress follows up with policy determinations that are based on the evidence presented. If the Congress acts on vague assumptions rather than substantive evidence, the power to set public policy will remain hidden from public view.

ROUND UP THE USUAL SUSPECTS

One of the critical questions facing Congress is the possibility of a game-changing terrestrial threat. The two most likely candidates are the People's Republic of China and the Russian Federation. Both are potential adversaries that would use a new weapon that provides a significant advantage. Instead, China has, until recently, conducted an inward looking foreign policy that attempts to consolidate economic gains before raising its military profile. Recent events demonstrate a policy shift towards a more aggressive foreign policy whether in the Taiwan Straits, Kashmir, or the Spratley Islands. Russia has been more aggressive in the last decade with its takeover of Crimea; conflict in the Ukraine; recently probing our defenses over Alaskan airspace; and its cybersecurity attacks. Could either of these countries have been secretly developing a new technology for which we have no defense? If so, why haven't they used this advantage?

Considering the timing of the incidents, starting with the Nimitz Carrier Group in 2004, it is highly unlikely that either country would have been in a position to develop objects with highly advanced technologies. China was concentrating on economic development after its 1978 transition to a more market-based economy. Russia, after the fall of the Soviet Union, fell into a depression and it took years for its oil-based economy to rebound. As with all resource-based economies,

Russia suffers from the ups and downs of the market. Neither China nor Russia had the resources to embark on massive Manhattan Project-style research and development programs needed to deploy the small fleet of objects seen by highly trained personnel.

Specifically, the Russian Federation, during the 1990s, was reeling from the collapse of the Soviet Union. While Western sources believed that the Soviet Union spent about 15% of the gross domestic product (GDP) on military expenditures, it was later learned that defense expenditures made up around 25% of its GDP. This underestimation of the drain on the economy of the U.S.S.R. was the main reason that Western intelligence agencies did not foresee its rapid collapse. After the collapse, Russian troops were not being paid, nuclear weapons were not being secured, and defense and industrial equipment was being cannibalized. The United States stepped in to help the Russians secure nuclear weapons to prevent their sale to other countries and terrorist groups. The Russian economy, with its overreliance on hydrocarbon exports, has waxed and waned with petroleum prices to this day. Despite claims by Vladimir Putin to the contrary, Russia is likely falling behind in weapons development rather than taking a great leap forward.

China has taken a different path. Market reforms have led to an increasingly consumption-based economy. However, while growing, its military expenditures were still far below the percentage of U.S. GDP spent on the military. In fact, the Chinese defense expenditures must also support a far larger land army. Their sophisticated weapons expenditures are dwarfed by the U.S. which relies heavily on technology. During the 26 years between the beginning of its market reforms and 2004, it is highly unlikely that research and development expenditures would have been made to achieve the type of technological breakthroughs needed to create the dozens of objects seen by naval personnel off the California Coast in November 2004.

For either Russia or China, the R & D requirements to develop and deploy dozens of ultra-high performance vehicles during the time window in question is simply beyond their capabilities. Consider the materials, propulsion system, and technological advances that are needed to be brought together to produce a single prototype of the Nimitz Carrier Group "tic tacs." Electronic records, currently held by some U.S. agency, and eyewitness accounts showed that there were "dozens" of these objects flying in formation. These objects performed impossible aerobatics while in formation. Even if a foreign power produced a prototype before November 2004, the public testimony shows that the number of craft and their performance characteristics must have been in service many years before the Nimitz encounters. To overcome these obstacles, classified information must show that either China or Russia diverted a significant portion of their GDP to secret projects involving exotic technologies. Given the development and testing needed to put multiple advanced craft into service by 2004, the terrestrial adversary possibility is not plausible. To advise Congress that one of these adversaries is the source of these objects, the DNI report's classified appendix would have to share information to overcome these apparent obstacles.

POTENTIAL NON-TERRESTRIAL CAUSE(S)

If evidence of a terrestrial source is lacking, the absence of evidence raises the possibility of a non-terrestrial cause. A report from the DNI that does not provide evidence of a source and asks for money to continue research keeps us in the same place we were in the 1950s. The Defense Department and intelligence agencies will be in control with no real congressional oversight. Merely throwing money at the problem will not make it go away.

Considering the vast technological gap between our current military forces and UFO/UAPs, it is possible that they are not terrestrial. If so, the technological gap may be measured in millions of years rather than decades. Unilateral, aggressive actions by the United States could create a larger problem than we have at the moment. Providing money to the defense and intelligence communities without oversight could lead to military confrontations triggering a greater conflict that we can't control. This is especially true under the current policy of keeping our frontline armed forces in the dark about this presence. Because of this secrecy, the chances of an accidental engagement are increased. It is possible that such engagements have already happened without congressional knowledge.

More information is needed to help Congress participate in long-term policy formulation. Congress needs to work with more than just three videos taken over the last 16 years. Both a broader group of experiences from our past interactions and those of other terrestrial actors must be drawn upon before taking any course of action with non-terrestrial possibilities still on the table. Lack of evidence of a terrestrial source that could develop and deploy the numbers of objects seen by the 2004 Nimitz Carrier Group means that our elected officials must be more involved rather the less. Seventy-plus years of experiences without congressional involvement appears to have done little to address this ultimate problem. Returning the "problem"[92] to the unelected will mean a few people, behind closed doors, may decide our fate.

First, we must look to an unvarnished history of this phenomenon to see what lessons could be learned. From the declassified record, it appears that close observation of our military operations has been occurring at least since World War II. In 1952, Captain Edward Ruppelt, Operation Blue Book, noticed that the UFO/UAP phenomenon took a particular interest in our military assets.[93] This interest included our above-ground nuclear tests.[94]

Once we developed ICBMs, missile silos became a focus of more than just observation. These sites attracted UFO/UAPs who demonstrated their ability to temporarily decommission both our nuclear weapons as well as those of our adversaries.[95] Congress must review this

---

92   Declassified CIA memos labeled the UFO/UAP issue as the "problem".

93   Ruppelt, Edward J., The Report on Unidentified Flying Objects (Original 1956 Edition) Doubleday & Company, reissued Cosimo Classics (2011), reprint of 1956 original version.

94   Hastings, Robert, UFOs and Nukes: Extraordinary Encounters at Nuclear Weapons Sites, AuthorHouse (2008), pp. 97–104.

95   Id. Salas, Robert & Klotz, James, Faded Giant, BookSurge, LLC (2005), pp. 12–27,44–45.

history, including classified materials, to determine the patterns and intent behind this conduct. Recommendations to the new presidential administration should include consultations with our allies regarding similar conduct.

From the declassified record, observation and development of the ability to interfere with nuclear weapon use are long-term activities of the intelligence(s) that control UFO/UAPs. Congress needs to see the classified records of military-UFO/UAP interactions to try to learn more about the ultimate motives of these visitors to our planet. From the declassified record, it is clear that more information on this issue is hidden.

Both from the timing of the presence of these objects during WWII and the actions they have taken, the focus on nuclear weapons is significant. It is a persistent part of this phenomenon. Is it because they are our only defense against a potential non-terrestrial occupying power? This seems unlikely given the 70-plus years this phenomenon has been present. Usually, an invading power does not give its adversary a 70-year head start to prepare a defense. However, the stakes are so high that the possibility cannot be completely dismissed. The difference between where we were technologically in the 1940s and today should provide some comfort about this possibility. After this passage of time, we should be more prepared even though a wide gap still exists.

Observation and selective acts of temporarily disarming a portion of our nuclear forces could also point to a possibility that is more benign. Consider our current stage of development. We are on the verge of space exploration and possess world-destroying weapons. This may alarm local neighbors who have already passed this stage of development. A much older civilization may be concerned with our aggressive behavior if we were to develop interstellar exploration, whether via probes or a human crew.

Concern of a nearby neighbor may not be a civilization in a local star system. The nearest neighbor may be occupying the same "space" as Earth in another dimension. The effects of a nuclear detonation may extend past the dimension we live in and cause harm to another. After all, our scientific knowledge is limited to the observable matter that only makes up less than five percent of the universe. The other 95% is made up of dark matter and dark energy. The need to monitor our nuclear weapons development and deployment may be about concern for nearby realms.

If there are more advanced civilizations observing Earth and taking defensive measures to protect themselves, who are they? It is likely not one civilization because of the variety of craft and related encounters. It is more likely that these visitors are from different planets and/or realms. If so, it is unlikely that they have the same purpose for being here. Some may be here for purely scientific purposes. Others may be here to take resources from the Earth and surrounding environs. The resources may include our planetary biodiversity, rare earths, or materials that we consider valueless, but are necessary for some advanced technological purpose. Perhaps, they are waiting for us to destroy ourselves. Looking at the evolution of our civilization and our current challenges, it is hardly a stretch that humanity may be unable to progress beyond the problems confronting us.

Many commentators speculate that any meeting we have with a far-superior civilization will mean the end of our civilization. The late Stephen Hawking considered this possibility. The 1960 Brookings Institute report to NASA about the implications of space travel echoed a similar concern. These concerns are mostly based on our experiences of colonization from the 15th century to the present. Yet, most social science researchers now point to the introduction of novel diseases to "less advanced" cultures were the primary cause of their decline. Smallpox alone subdued more populations than all military conquests.[96]

A better example to call upon is one involving a socially developed, but technologically backward culture. The Meiji Restoration changed

---

96   Hopkins, Donald, The Greatest Killer: Smallpox in History, The University of Chicago Press (2002); Diamond, Jared, Guns, Germs, and Steel: The Fates of Human Societies, W.W. Norton & Company (1997), p. 197.

Japan and helped it become a modern, industrialized country.[97] In the 19th century, Japan was an isolated, feudal society that was ruled by warlords (shogunate). This form of government began in the 17th century when, after a long period of warfare, the emperor was reduced to a figurehead. The shogunate kept Japan isolated from the outside world, which stifled its technological development. In 1853, Commodore Mathew Perry sailed a flotilla of ironclad warships into what is now called Tokyo Bay. The technological gap between the feudal Japanese and this new threat was staggering. This show of strength forced Japan to sign trade agreements with the United States and European powers. To the Japanese, the technological gap appeared massive.

Instead of collapsing Japanese society, this shock brought a new resolve. In 1868, the feudal system gave way to a restoration of power to the emperor. This change helped consolidate power and allow for greater development in a society that turned away from its feudalistic past. Japanese society remade itself but kept its cultural identity intact. Many of its citizens began studying abroad and gave the country a new class of highly-educated engineers and other professionals that helped Japan to turn itself into a more industrialized society on par with the Western world. Unfortunately, much of its efforts were channeled into military expansionism. Yet today, Japan is a world economic power with its unique culture intact.

Because of earlier sporadic contact with mainland Asia, Japan had suffered through a smallpox epidemic in 735–737 A.D. that killed about one-third of its population.[98] While it had further outbreaks thereafter, it had built up immunities so that Commodore Perry's visits did not cause the same type of devastation occurring during other clashes of cultures. Most notably, European expansionism beginning in the 15th century. Today, the arrival of UFO/UAPs has not led to the same kind of exotic disease outbreaks that have crippled or destroyed so

---

97   Ravina, Mark, To Stand with the Nations of the World: Japan's Meiji Restoration in World History, Oxford University Press (2007).

98   Hopkins, Donald, The Greatest Killer: Smallpox in History, The University of Chicago Press (2002) pp. 106–109.

many civilizations on Earth. If there are interactions between our civilization and non-terrestrial ones since at least World War II, they haven't spread off-planet novel diseases. This can be attributed to the fact that a highly advanced civilization would take precautions to protect all parties unless it intentionally wanted to introduce a deadly pathogen. If it had, we would not be here today.

The 19th century Meiji Restoration is the example that more closely fits our current situation. Coming into contact with a more advanced civilization caused Japan to make societal changes that allowed it to compete in a new world. Just as feudal Japan recognized the challenges and adapted, so can our world society if faced with a similar challenge. However, one must first recognize the situation that we are facing. Making these types of changes will not happen without public knowledge of the situation. As it is difficult for our frontline military forces to adapt when they are unaware of the potential challenge they face, the same can be said of the American people. They cannot adapt unless they know why they are adapting. It also requires trust in their leadership to help guide the way. If a non-terrestrial challenge is waiting for us, keeping it secret will make the eventual transition more difficult.

The alternative is to return the issue to the clandestine world where decisions will be made from a narrower perspective. Defense and intelligence interests will prevail with the larger perspective ignored. This scenario has happened before. In early August 1952, President Harry Truman asked the CIA to look into the UFO/UAP issue after an alarming set of incidents over the restricted airspace of Washington D.C. on two successive weekends in late July 1952. Within three weeks, the CIA, in consultation with the Air Force, determined to see if UFO/UAPs could be used as either an offensive or defensive propaganda weapon against the Soviet Union. According to declassified records, these early meetings focused on the people who have seen or those who study UFO/UAPs, rather than the objects themselves. Without evidence, Air Force personnel claimed that some flying saucer groups had "questionable loyalties." These August meetings set in motion a process that took the study away from Truman's request to study the phenomenon and turned the Robertson Panel into one that questioned those who had seen or had studied UFO/UAPs. Without appropriate oversight, the process became one that sought to limit interest in the subject rather than try to understand it.

Even if there are reasons to keep UFO/UAP study in the classified world, hidden from Congress, this policy narrows the ability of the federal government to see a broader picture. Since the 1980s, social science research has helped us understand how to improve public policy decision-making.[99] Many decisions are made by persons with identical viewpoints and interests. This research shows that, the more a group of decision-makers have in common, the more likely that their decisions will ignore evidence that does not agree with their pre-set notions. Groupthink can serve to reinforce prejudices, preconceived notions, and to ignore contrary evidence. Whether the studies involved juries, public bodies, or business decisions, a greater range of opinions and perspectives improved the quality of group decision-making.[100]

Unless the outcome of the DNI's report and congressional committee follow up inquiries is that the UFO/UAP phenomenon only has a terrestrial source, Congress should expand the inquiry into a broader review. Different perspectives and continued congressional oversight will help Congress see the bigger picture. This phenomenon has cultural, governmental, and broader societal implications that should not be determined by a narrow band of officials with defense-only interests. Perhaps the history of UFO/UAP observation and nuclear interference is a real threat to humanity. Or perhaps not. Foreclosing a broader area of inquiry by sending the issue back to the classified world could have long-term negative consequences for the United States and humanity in general.

---

99 Stangor, Dr. Charles, Jhangiani, Dr. Rajiv, & Tarry, Dr. Hammond, Principles of Social Psychology - 1st International Edition, BCC Campus, p. 481 et. seq. (Ch. 10 Group Decision-Making).

100 Sommers, S. R., "On racial diversity and group decision-making: Identifying multiple effects of racial composition on jury deliberations," Journal of Personality and Social Psychology, vol. 90, pp. 597–612; Reagans, Ray, In Search of Significance: A Role-Set Approach to Uncovering the Social Importance of Demographic Categories, Phillips, Katherine, Diversity and Groups, JAI Press (2008), pp. 93–108.

The timing of the Senate Select Intelligence Committee referral of this issue is interesting. It has happened in the middle of a global pandemic with the country having undergone a traumatic election and the worst combination of weather disasters in modern memory. Questions are being raised about the fairness of our society. These are all issues that deserve serious attention. However, time is running out for delaying a broader inquiry into the UFO/UAP phenomenon. On October 31, 2021, the James Webb Space Telescope will be launched by NASA. From its platform a million miles above Earth, it will see farther and with more detail into the cosmos than we ever have. One of its missions will be to look for exoplanets and signs of life. Confirmation that we are not alone in the universe may come before the end of the 117th Congress. Signs of advanced civilizations could also be on our telescope's horizon.

As each new discovery is announced, the recognition of intelligent life will open up discussion of possible non-terrestrial presence on Earth. Considering society's accelerating pace of acceptance of a new idea once it has begun to trend, acceptance of the idea that Earth is being visited by intelligent civilizations will likely come quickly. The question will be whether our elected leaders will be a proactive part of the solution rather than being seen as resisting change even as evidence mounts.

How Congress acts on this referral to four of its most important public policy committees could have historical significance. The report requested in the committee comments attached to the FY 2021 Intelligence Authorization Act could begin an iterative process that charts a course for humanity as it reaches beyond this world. The question of the millennium could be answered in the near future. True leadership will be needed to help guide us towards a new world.

CPSIA information can be obtained
at www.ICGtesting.com
Printed in the USA
FSHW010652290321

9 781977 240903